D1534746

BELIEF

BELIEF

Form, Content, and Function

EDITED BY
RADU J. BOGDAN

CLARENDON PRESS · OXFORD
1986

Oxford University Press, Walton Street, Oxford OX2 6DP

Oxford New York Toronto
Delhi Bombay Calcutta Madras Karachi
Petaling Jaya Singapore Hong Kong Tokyo
Nairobi Dar es Salaam Cape Town
Melbourne Auckland

and associated companies in
Beirut Berlin Ibadan Nicosia

Oxford is a trade mark of Oxford University Press

Published in the United States
by Oxford University Press, New York

British Library Cataloguing in Publication Data

Belief: form, content and function.
1. Belief and doubt
I. Bogdan, Radu J.
121'.6 BD215

ISBN 0–19–824758–3
ISBN 0–19–824745–1 Pbk

Library of Congress Cataloging-in-Publication Data

Belief: form, content, and function.
Includes indexes.
1. Belief and doubt. I. Bogdan, Radu J.
BD215.B44 1986 121'.6 86–8677

ISBN 0–19–824758–3
ISBN 0–19–824745–1 (pbk.)

Set by Wyvern Typesetting Limited, Bristol
Printed in Great Britain
at the University Printing House, Oxford
by David Stanford
Printer to the University

CONTENTS

CONTRIBUTORS

RADU J. BOGDAN. Assistant Professor of Philosophy, Tulane University, New Orleans. Editor of *Profiles: An International Series on Contemporary Philosophers and Logicians* and author of articles on philosophy of mind, epistemology, and inductive logic.

FRED DRETSKE. Professor of Philosophy, University of Wisconsin, Madison. Author of *Seeing and Knowing* (1969) and *Knowledge and the Flow of Information* (1981).

KEITH LEHRER. Professor of Philosophy, University of Arizona. Author of *Knowledge* (1974) and co-author with Carl Wagner of *Rational Consensus in Science and Society* (1981).

WILLIAM G. LYCAN. Professor of Philosophy, University of North Carolina at Chapel Hill. Author of *Logical Form in Natural Language* (1984) and co-author with Steven Boër of *Knowing Who* (1985).

STEPHEN SCHIFFER. Professor of Philosophy, University of Arizona. Author of *Meaning* (1972).

STEPHEN P. STICH. Professor of Philosophy, University of Maryland. Author of *From Folk Psychology to Cognitive Science: The Case Against Belief* (1983) and co-editor with David A. Jackson of *The Recombinant DNA Debate* (1978).

CHAPTER I

THE IMPORTANCE OF BELIEF

RADU J. BOGDAN

I. THE ISSUE

Once upon a time there was a mighty firm called Cognikos, famous maker of intelligent systems. The firm was located in the heart of a mighty and famous area of Mars called Sillyclon Valley. The crack research team at the firm was working on a top-priority project dubbed EI (for Earthly Intelligence). The Martian researchers had never had any personal contact with earthly humans but knew a lot about them. The Martians had pictures of films about humans, and copies of major books and papers in neuroscience and psychology written by famous humans; and they had even managed to get a human brain for detailed study. Such, then, was the data base for the EI research at Cognikos. After a good beginning and some steady progress in understanding how humans perceive and use language and even solve fairly simple problems, the Martian team began to face increasing difficulties in deciphering and modelling more complex cognitive functions of the earthly mind. After a while, they decided that something important was missing from their picture. At their mid-morning meeting the EI researchers were 'brainstorming' each other furiously, to no avail.

'Look,' they told the vice-president in charge of the project, 'we have pretty much figured out how, at a basic level, humans absorb, represent, and use information. In fact, it appears that towards the end of the twentieth century the humans themselves began to understand some of their basic perceptual and linguistic capabilities. But obviously this is not enough. More complex cognition, in the human case, does not appear to flow from simpler structures, as it does in our case. We are not designed the same way. So we have a problem.'

Exasperated, the vice-president summoned Doxoi, the firm's top intellectual spy. 'Doxoi,' the vice-president said, 'we are going to send you on a mission to Earth. Keep your eyes wide open, sniff around, listen a lot, read their academic and non-academic output, talk even to the lovers of wisdom, and try to find out what we are missing from the story of human cognition. And Doxoi? Bring me a hamburger and a Coke from down there, will you?'

So off went Doxoi. He listened to, and taped, countless academic talks and ordinary conversations in various earthly languages, read all sorts of things, went to many lectures and seminars all over the planet, and kept his eyes and ears open. Satisfied that he had gathered a fairly extensive body of information on EI, he went to see the man down south, after which he returned to Mars.

At the Monday meeting they were all impatient. 'I have good news and bad news,' said Doxoi. 'The good news is that I may have found what we are looking for, the missing link in our picture of EI. The bad news is that I do not know what to make of the good news and, I am afraid, nor will you. I begin with the good news.

'As you well know, like us, humans register, represent, store, and use information. Some of their information processes, like all of ours, are rigidly programmed, or modular, in their entirety. But others, apparently, are not. Also, whereas we have a lot of modules, they seem to have only a few. When they go beyond the range of the modules, which is quite often, they somehow improvise. This is probably why, unlike us, humans seem to hesitate a lot, if "hesitate" is the right word. It is a strange phenomenon but quite prevalent down there They even seem to enjoy it. Weird. Anyway, there, I think, may be the key to our problem.

'First, I looked for the linguistic evidence, which, indeed, seems to support the centrality of hesitation in their cognitive life. For example, all their languages seem to have words like "believe", "assume", "imagine", 'guess". And they use such words quite a lot, particularly in situations which fit my hypothesis about their cognitive hesitation. From now on I will take the generic word "belief" to stand for the class of human words used in those situations. So, my hypothesis is: whatever the notion of belief is, it may solve our problem.

'Once this became clear to me, I started looking for what humans had to say about the notion of belief. This is where the good news tends to slide into bad news. It turns out that only their philosophers are genuinely interested in the notion. Their cognitive psychologists and brain scientists show no such interest, which is why we found nothing in their literature. (Some humans seem to think that psychologists and brain scientists do, in fact, deal with this notion of belief, but in terms of more basic processes. I wasn't able to find any evidence to this effect.) But, even with the philosophers, the situation is not that simple. It seems, from what I could gather in my travels, that only the English-speaking philosophers worry and write extensively about belief. (Pain is another thing they worry and write a lot about, but that is another matter. Or is it?) Anyway, for reasons which I couldn't really fathom, European, Russian, and other species of philosophers do not seem excited by the topic of belief. This may be significant, but I did not have time to pursue the matter. There is, however, one linguistic detail I thought you people might want to know about. "Belief" in English appears to be more versatile, and in some sense more neutral, than in, say, French or German. In the latter languages "belief" is truly synonymous with "opinion", "conviction", and the like. What is interesting is that English allows you to speak (in a philosophical tone of voice) of, say, "animal belief" or "perceptual belief". In French, I am told, *opinion animale* or *croyance perceptuelle* sounds a bit odd, if not plain silly. A French sage is said to have said, *Avoir une opinion, c'est préférer de se tromper*. Modules do not have this option. Not on the continent of Europe, anyway. It seems that in some languages you cannot easily attribute belief to simple information processors. There may be a correlation between what a language allows you to say about belief and what you say philosophically about belief in that language.

'Perhaps this would not matter too much if it were not for the following important fact. It appears that from their early antiquity until early in the twentieth century earthly philosophers had no hesitation about putting forward bold, venturesome theories about this or that topic without worrying about common sense or linguistic practices—in fact, they enjoyed challenging them. Whether right or wrong, at least they knew what they wanted and what they were after. In particular, no theory of the mind from Plato to Descartes to Kant to Husserl had much to do with earthly common sense and the way *hoi polloi* speak. But, for a number of reasons, this has changed in the last decades of the twentieth century. Philosophical populism, or *hoi polloi*-ism (meaning what people say and do in normal life), and personal intuitions are now very fashionable. The result is that philosophers no longer have bold, venturesome, even a priori ideas about a phenomenon like belief, the way Plato had. What many philosophers are doing these days is polling each other and the man in the street for their raw, basic "intuitions" (they talk of "intuitions" all the time!), on which they then build rather non-intuitive technical analyses. The results are not always very enlightening, I must say. So this may be as good a moment as any to take a quick look at the philosophical picture of belief. Now you will understand the sense of "bad news". I will start with a graphic schematization (Figure 1) and then amplify a bit. The aim is to give you the main options with their pluses and minuses, so you can apply a cost-benefit analysis.

'The first bifurcation is the toughest for us. If belief is nothing, that is, if the notion of belief describes nothing in the mind, then we cannot expect that notion to give us the key to human cognition. Now why would enlightened people down there say that belief was nothing, which would mean that it had nothing concrete in it, or that it should not be construed realistically, or that it could not be mapped on to distinguishable and autonomous cognitive mechanisms, structures, or processes, or, in general, that the notion of belief was not psychologically or neuroscientifically or even physically descriptive? Let us call philosophers who take this line, in different versions, "belief eliminativists". What are the appeal of and the reasons for such eliminativism? One idea, popular some time ago, is that talk of belief is just a matter of linguistic practice and usage, a way of saying something appropriate in certain circumstances, for instance, when one wants to indicate hesitation or uncertainty or a certain logical treatment of a sentence (one says "I believe that p" to indicate "I take p as a premiss", or the like). This, I thought, sounds fine, but why would humans *want* or *need* to talk that way in the first place; what is the *rationale* behind their linguistic practices? Interestingly, many philosophers who subscribe to this socio-linguistic elimination of belief do not ask these prior and deeper questions. They just describe the phenomenon without explaining it. They may say, for example, that it is their language game or that they have been conditioned by society to talk that way. Notice that in a sense these philosophers are realists about belief. They imply that talk of belief describes certain configurations of social, practical, and communicational circumstances. But that is not going to help us, because we want to design an intelligent human mind, not (thank God) an intelligent human society.

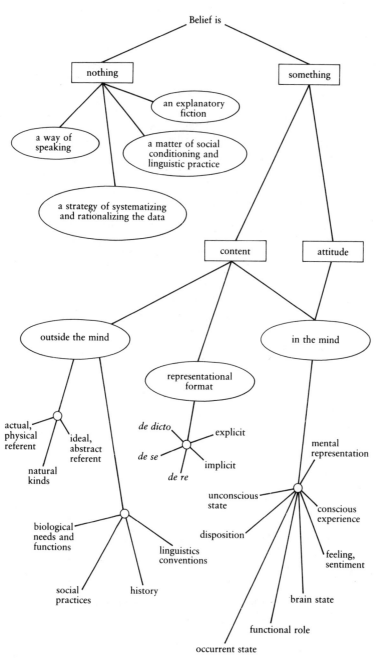

Fig. 1.

'Another group of belief eliminativists, the strategic eliminativists, holds the view that talk of belief is a useful conceptual strategy in terms of which we can systematize, rationalize, and predict at some appropriate level of abstraction (which they typically call "intentional"), what humans say and do. When (they argue) we look more closely at how the mind instantiates or executes the intentionally attributed beliefs and other mental attitudes, we must realize that all we are going to find are fairly simple, non-intelligent, non-intentional microsystems which do their job—a job which we can describe, at a lower level, symbolically and computationally, and, at a still lower level, biochemically or something like that. Belief, as an autonomous notion, evaporates when we so slide down this explanatory slope.

'Ferocious eliminativism is the last version I want to mention. Those who take this line find talk of belief not only metaphysically empty but intellectually dangerous and useless. To them, talk of belief is just a residue of a stubborn Neanderthal myth, a sort of alchemy or astrology of the mind, which completely misdescribes the mental life of humans and is incapable of explaining, causally, even the most elementary cognitive accomplishments. With time and adequate funding, it is expected, this myth will be entirely replaced by the advancing neurosciences. So much, then, about the many ways in which belief is nothing.'

At this point the EI project vice-president raised his hand. 'Is there any chance,' he asked, 'that these eliminativists take the human mind to be much more modular than we think? The nothingness of belief would suit us well *if* humans were modular, as we are. But we think they are not modular, which is why they hesitate, which is why they believe. One may of course stipulate belief out of existence but that would not solve our problem, which is the problem of their cognitive "hesitation", as you call it. Even if one eliminates belief, one must, at some point, invent another notion to deal with cognitive hesitation, if the latter is a real phenomenon. So, my question really is: how do eliminativists handle cognitive hesitation?'

'Good question,' said Doxoi. 'I don't know. I'm not even sure that the eliminativists are all aware of the problem. The ferocious ones certainly aren't. The socio-linguistic eliminativists tend to shift the problem from the individual mind to society and its linguistic habits. I wouldn't be surprised if they said that humans were socially conditioned to hesitate. ("Belief", they may say, "is what society tells you to hesitate about." The strategic eliminativists may recognize the problem and the social strategies for dealing with it (rational calculus of probabilities and utilities and the like), but, in a way I cannot fully understand, they hope that in the long run a sort of modular psychology and neuroscience will do all the explaining. Good luck. Any further questions?

'All right, then. Now the other major alternative. Belief is something, that is, something mental. What exactly? Well, the current consensus within that alternative is that, at the very least, belief must be a mental attitude to a representational content, specifically, to whatever the content clause "that *p*" stands for in "S believes that *p*". The content must have a propositional format because it represents not objects or properties as such but, rather, facts about them. This is where the consensus ends and the frustration begins.

'About the attitude itself there is not very much to say. It looks like a rather thin notion. Very early in the philosophical game, the attitude had been characterized as, for example, a capacity directed towards certain aspects of the world and responsible for producing certain specific cognitive experiences. That, I was told, was Plato's view. There is, to my mind, an interesting reading of the subsequent development of the notion of belief. It looks as though each of the two components of the Platonic view, the capacity and the resulting cognitive experience, became an independent and self-sufficient candidate for the notion of belief. The notion of capacity resurfaces in modern times as the notion of belief as disposition. The cognitive experience, on the other hand, resurfaces in such modern notions as belief as conscious experience, or feeling, or sentiment, or vivid mental representation, or the like. The dispositional notion is attractive to the more scientifically and behaviouristically inclined philosophers, the notion of conscious experience to the more introspective or mentalist philosophers. As far as I can tell, neither notion is very promising. Surely, believing must involve a disposition or capacity, but so do many other mental attitudes and undertakings. A specific disposition to act in response to an input? This must be true of desires and intentions as well. Also, overt action cannot be the only manifestation of belief. A belief may also be responsible for, and hence manifested by, other beliefs and mental attitudes, inferences, and so on. If we want to design such a disposition, the dispositionalist literature is not going to be of much help. Nor are we going to be much better off with the notion of belief as conscious experience. For one thing, I could not tell from the literature on this subject whether, when talking of a conscious experience, philosophers were talking of belief itself, or of a result of believing, hence of the evidence for believing. The notion fits both these readings too well to be of much use. Another handicap is that the notion of conscious experience cannot accommodate unconscious belief, a phenomenon that humans have come to accept, rather reluctantly, in recent times.

'An apparently more promising notion explicates the attitude part of belief as functional role. A mental content, on this notion, is a belief only if it plays a role in the organism's cognition and behaviour. That is all right, but it does not take us much further than the earlier, dispositionalist idea. It may be that now the belief is not so much the disposition but its exercise in certain conditions. But, somehow, it looks like the same general slogan. Yet, it should be said, both the notion of belief as disposition and that of belief as functional role have the quality of emphasizing that an inert mental content will not do. Unfortunately, so far, they fail to specify concrete constraints on what makes mental representations operate in executive positions.

'There is one more complication on the attitude side of the belief question. It has to do with the traditional human expectation that beliefs come in degrees. Humans' ordinary doxastic vocabulary is very sensitive to this expectation. There are even ordinary as well as sophisticated ways—betting, for example—of measuring the strength of one's beliefs. So we may have to think of incorporating a probability metric in our doxastic concoction. There are fierce disagreements among philosophers down there about how to construe this probability metric of belief, but I will let this pass. Those interested can read the literature I have brought with me. The problem I want to address myself to is this: there is a vocal minority, both in epistemology and philosophy of science, which argues that belief is, in some sense, an absolute, all-or-nothing notion, not a probabilistic one. One interesting reason in support of this view is connected with the idea of belief as functional role. It is said that a belief must be treated as certain, with probability one, if it is to play a role in either cognition or behaviour. For example, the argument goes, a belief could not be a premiss in an argument if it was not premissed as true. Even if the premissing is conditional, as it most often is, the probability of the premiss is still one *in that context*. Likewise, a belief cannot support an intention or an action if, at least in that context, it is not treated as true. It appears, then, that dogmatism of belief, however contextual, must go hand in hand with a belief playing a functional role. Revision of belief, on this view, is not revision of probabilities but, rather, a qualitative change of mind. What about probabilistic belief? I have a suspicion that it must be relegated to the modular formation of formal representations, but that, for many people, is not fixation of belief. Given the way we Martians function, we must agree, mustn't we?' (Uncomfortable laughter in the audience.)

'What about belief content? Well, the story gets rather complicated at this point. A belief content is, first of all, a mental representation, whether a visual image or a sentence in some natural language. There is also talk down there of an inner code, or language, of mental representation, underlying the various surface representations I have just enumerated. If so, then a belief is ultimately a relation to some formal structure in this basic code. Whatever the code in which a mental form gets expressed, the question we want to ask is, what exactly is it that a mental form encodes or represents? That is, what sorts of constraints must the encoding or representation comply with? For example, if syntactic constraints are the only constraints on encoding, then a belief content is a mere syntactic form. Some theorists down there are prepared to claim precisely this. But most appear to think that this is insufficient, and that additional, meaning-determining constraints are also needed. In that case, a belief content is a meaning*ful* syntactic form of some sort. The emphasis being on the natural language, a belief content is typically a sentence in some such language. Perhaps the philosophical notion that best captures this construing of belief content as a meaningful form is that of proposition.

'How are they construing such meanings or propositions? With anarchic gusto. For some, propositions or meanings are only in the head, for example, as syntactic forms under concepts. For others, what is in the head is not enough to fix a meaning or a proposition. External, non-mental co-ordinates are also needed. These co-ordinates may be abstract and ideal, as in the Plato–Frege tradition, or particular and physical, as in the Russell tradition, or, finally, "natural-kind-ish" and physical, as in the more recent Putnam–Kripke tradition. For still others, all these co-ordinates are still insufficient to characterize the aboutness of belief. Linguistic conventions and social practices must also get into the picture, with the consequence that what people are conditioned or used to saying in a given linguistic community is going to affect *what* they think and believe, or perhaps the way we should construe and explain what they think and believe. This in turn reinforces the view that belief is not a purely cognitive notion or, from an explanatory viewpoint, not a pure psychological construct.'

'Freeze right where you are!' urged a young researcher. 'Let us assume that propositions, as meanings, are not only in the head. Let us also assume that beliefs are entirely in the head, that is, mental forms with an internal role. Wouldn't this indicate that what is believed is not necessarily a proposition or meaning?'

'Elementary, my dear Watson,' smiled Doxoi. 'That is indeed an attractive possibility, if one *also* happens to think that logical and semantic criteria are not psychologically explanatory. The notion of proposition is indeed a creature of logical and semantic constraints. We notice, therefore, that the notion of belief is pulled in two opposite directions. On the one hand, if the notion of belief is to explain what is going on in the mind, then apparently it cannot explain what is objectively believed. This in turn seems to undermine the very possibility of public and objective attribution of belief. On the other hand, if we want to protect the latter possibility, we have to make assumptions, like the semantic and logical ones, which do not have psychological cash value. A choice has to be made.'

Another Martian hand was trying to catch Doxoi's attention. 'How did they get into this mess about meanings and beliefs inside and outside the head?'

'It is hard to tell,' sighed Doxoi. 'Probably a combination of several developments. One I noticed is the vigorous, and now fashionable, emergence of naturalism in philosophy of mind, language, and epistemology. The general naturalist slogan is that the head is a part of the world, so to understand what is in the head is to understand what external inputs reach the head. Another development has to do with the very mechanism which accounts for how the world influences what goes on in the head. Generically speaking, it is causation. Causal theories are meant to characterize what various types of mental states are about, irrespective of how those states represent what they are about. Philosophers now have causal theories for everything—you name it, perception, memory, knowledge, reference, and, of course, belief. But do not ask me the antecedent question, why naturalism and causation? I gather it is a long story, a sort of radical reaction to mentalism and Cartesianism, which always leave an unbridgeable gap between the mind and the world. Why unbridgeable? Because any contact with the world is representational, so you can't get out of the circle of representations—out of the head, that is—to establish the aboutness of the representations and check how well they represent what they do. That is the rough idea. Therefore, instead of playing this exclusively representational game, the naturalist says: "I am going to establish both the aboutness of a representation and its cognitive reliability by looking at how the representation is formed, in particular the causal mechanisms of that formation." Genetic fallacy? Maybe. There is finally the development already mentioned which says that social and language games, hence factors external to the mind, shape the contents of human thoughts, beliefs, and speech acts.

'Now one point that has to be noticed is that the external determinants of content and belief, whether causal or social or whatever, are not necessarily represented in the mind. They shape content without being explicitly encoded in it. This is the fact, I take it, behind the distinction between beliefs *de re* and beliefs *de dicto*. This is a distinction operative in occurrent contexts of cognition and generated by a question like: is a content fully mentalized and explicitly represented in the head? Hence should we represent it as the cognizer does, or should we add aspects to that content which the cognizer does not necessarily represent? But there is a more general, non-occurrent moral to this externalist story. It seems to say that contents and beliefs are shaped by deeper, more enduring, and latent external factors, such as environment, social and linguistic community, the history of the organisms in question, and the like.'

'We should be better off with Cartesian mentalism, if we want to simulate human cognition and belief, shouldn't we? It is a simpler and more elegant hypothesis.' The voice was timid, but many were nodding in approval.

'That is true,' said Doxoi, 'assuming that mentalism is right. Unfortunately, truth is often very messy. But do not despair. There are still some valiant and bold mentalists down there who give the naturalists a hell of a fight. I have brought you some mentalist literature. Fun to read, no doubt about that.

'Well, I suppose that will do for this morning. There certainly are many others puzzles about belief. Are all beliefs explicitly represented and stored? Are all beliefs linguistic? Can animals believe? Believe what? How many beliefs can the mind hold? If only a few, in what sense are the rest beliefs? As implicit or tacit or virtual beliefs? What would those be? And then there are plenty of problems about the logical and semantic properties of the belief locutions. But I thought you needed first a general familiarization with the phenomenon of belief itself. As I said, I have brought with me plenty of literature. Tonight I will hold an informal seminar about the literature, as it relates to my presentation.

'I do not want to conclude, however, without mentioning a disturbing story which, I hope, will motivate you to work hard and unlock the mystery of human belief. Just as I was about to leave the world of belief down there, I chanced upon an article by D. K. Lewis called "Mad Pain and Martian Pain". Needless to say, I did not like the title. But I liked even less what came after the title. Let me quote the key passage about the Martian:

His hydraulic mind contains nothing like our neurons. Rather, there are various amounts of fluid in many inflatable cavities, and the inflation of any one of these cavities opens some valves and closes others. His [*he still means our, mind you*] mental plumbing pervades most of his body—in fact, all but the heat exchanger inside his head.

'I was really mad and pained, our good old Martian way, of course. As far as I can tell, it may be Lewis and his colleagues who have hydraulic minds, with their blood circulating in those tubes and all the rest. Remember Thales? More serious, though, is the implication of this misrepresentation of our beloved and efficient mind. If they think we have a hydraulic mind, they will also think we have some kind of fluid cognition. And then they will say that this is why we do not have beliefs and do not understand what it is to have a belief. Their reasoning is going to be as follows. Intelligent cognition requires digital and symbolic encoding and processing of information. Whatever is fluid is analog. Whatever is analog is physical, hence not mental. *Ergo*, Martians do not have minds. We've got to stop this nonsense before they become aware of it.

Our work on belief may dramatically alter this misperception. The question of belief is one of the toughest philosophical questions which humans have ever encountered. If we figure it out before they do, we surely must have minds.'

2. THE LITERATURE

'Welcome back. You have to understand, my non-hydraulic friends, that this is going to be just an informal, and not very representative, sampling of the earthly literature on belief. Just a beginning. No claim to completeness and objectivity is being made. I have selected some writings on the basis of both what human philosophers have told me and what I have read and heard. I concentrate on the topics I have talked about this morning.

'To begin with, I was not able to find one major, comprehensive, and recent monograph on belief. The only work I know which comes close to being such a monograph is H. H. Price's *Belief* (London, 1969). It is a work very much concerned with the classic mentalist and dispositionalist analyses of belief but much weaker on current trends and issues. Price's own view, an interesting version of traditional mentalism, is concisely presented in his "Some Considerations about Belief", *Proceedings of the Aristotelian Society*, 35 (1934–5), reprinted in A. Griffiths, *Knowledge and Belief* (Oxford UP, 1967).

'For various specific views on belief, let us go back to our earlier discussion and the tree diagram used then. I begin with the left-hand, belief-is-nothing position. First, socio-linguistic eliminativism. The ordinary (English) language philosophy best exemplifies this version of eliminativism. Two lively, imaginative, and durable papers, one by John Austin, "Other Minds", first published in the *Proceedings of the Aristotelian Society*, 20 (1946) and reprinted in his *Philosophical Papers* (Oxford UP, 3rd edn., 1979), the other by James Urmson, "Parenthetical Verbs", first published in *Mind*, 61 (1952), are probably the best guides to this line of thought. Wittgenstein's *On Certainty* (Oxford, 1969) may well be your next, and more esoteric, reading. Let your imagination read between the lines as well.

'Strategic eliminativism? Dennett's *Brainstorms* (Montgomery, Vt., 1978) is the book to read. There are traces of such eliminativism in some of Davidson's writings, now collected in two handy

volumes, *Essays on Actions and Events* (Oxford UP, 1980), particularly essays 11–14, and *Inquiries into Truth and Interpretation*
(Oxford UP, 1984), particularly essays 9–11. Stephen Stich's *From
Folk Psychology to Cognitive Science: The Case Against Belief* (MIT
Press, 1983) can be profitably read in the light of strategic
eliminativism, although many of its conclusions cannot be easily
classified in one slot or another. Paul Churchland may well be the
most ferocious of belief eliminativists in his *Scientific Realism and
the Plasticity of Mind* (Cambridge UP, 1979).

'Now, the positive literature on belief. Plato, I was told, develops
his pioneering views on belief in a number of his works. The notion
of belief mentioned in my talk is outlined in book V of his *Republic*.
From reports I had about the *Republic* we ought to read the whole
book, because it appears to have anticipated many aspects of our
beloved society. Plato may have failed to realize that modularity of
mind is a condition of knowledge (in his sense) and hence a
condition of being a philosopher-boss. Moreover, we have an
interesting social consequence of the phenomenon of belief. An
ideal Platonic society goes hand in hand with total modularity of
mind and knowledge. Democracy, on the other hand, appears to be
the political form which is best suited for people troubled by
cognitive hesitation, that is, believers. Blessed are those who do not
believe. But I digress.

'The mentalist, conscious-experience view of belief can be found
in a number of modern philosophers, most notably Hume and Reid,
and, in more recent times, Bertrand Russell in, say, his *Analysis of
Mind* (New York, 1921) and Price in the article mentioned at the
beginning of this talk. A classic and well defended statement of the
dispositionalist position is R. B. Braithwaite, "The Nature of
Believing", *Proceedings of the Aristotelian Society*, 33 (1932–3),
reprinted in Griffiths, *Knowledge and Belief*. And do not forget
Gilbert Ryle's *The Concept of Mind* (New York, 1949). Pure
delight. They do not write like this any more. Belief as functional
role is, as I said, more a slogan than a detailed analysis. So you find
this notion all over the place. For a clear and concise discussion of it,
try Gilbert Harman, *Thought* (Princeton UP, 1973).

'Now, probabilistic versus dogmatic belief. The notion that belief
is probabilistic goes back many centuries. An original and highly
readable history of probable belief (or opinion) and related notions
such as evidence, induction, and probability is Ian Hacking's *The*

Emergence of Probability (Cambridge UP, 1975). Pascal may have been the first philosopher to attempt to give a rigorous quantification of the strength of belief. I was pleased to stumble upon a now familiar method of measuring the probability of a belief in Kant's *Critique of Pure Reason*, about A824/B852. There is even a reading of Kant which may suggest the distinction we were talking about between probabilistic belief (covering both what he calls "pragmatic" belief and what he calls "doctrinal" belief) and dogmatic belief (his "moral belief"). The recent literature on inductive logic is mostly devoted to probabilistic belief, particularly in statistical practice and in science. The minority view which holds that the notion of dogmatic belief is needed to understand the role of belief in inquiry, deliberation, and action has been anticipated in some pragmatist writings and in some of Karl Popper's works. But the most consistent and systematic effort of articulating and defending the notion of dogmatic belief in inquiry and deliberation ("acceptance", as he calls it) that I know is Isaac Levi's in his *Gambling With Truth* (New York, 1967) and *The Enterprise of Knowledge* (MIT Press, 1980). In philosophy of mind, the distinction between dogmatic and probabilistic belief appears in Ronald de Sousa, "How To Give a Piece of Your Mind", *Review of Metaphysics*, 25 (1971), 52–79, and is further discussed by Dennett in *Brainstorms*, pp. 300–9.

'Belief content now. Stich's book *From Folk Psychology to Cognitive Science* gives probably the most comprehensive and careful overview of the various theories of belief content in current use. The notion that belief is a computational relation to a formula in an inner language of mental representation and that, therefore, a belief content is an exclusively syntactic construct is best articulated and rationalized by Jerry Fodor in his *Language of Thought* (Harvard UP, 1975) and *RePresentations* (MIT Press, 1981). The notion of belief content as a meaningful sentence in some natural language is quite widespread. The problem here, as mentioned in my talk this morning, is that there are many different, and often conflicting, theories of proposition or meaning as belief content. The literature is immense and grows monthly. (I wish some cool, tenured heads down there would urge a moratorium for some years.) So, instead of sampling the literature for you, I would rather recommend Dennett's own survey of it in "Beyond Belief", in A. Woodfield (ed.), *Thought and Object* (Oxford UP, 1982). Only let me mention that the tension in the current notion of belief between its psychological (in the head) and semantic (outside the head) dimensions is originally defined and analysed in Putnam's "The Meaning of 'Meaning' ", in K. Gunderson (ed.), *Minnesota Studies in the Philosophy of Science*, Vol. 7 (University of Minn. Press, 1975) reprinted in his *Philosophical Papers*, Vol. 2 (Cambridge UP 1975), and Fodor's "Methodological Solipsism Considered as a Research Strategy in Cognitive Psychology", *The Behavioral and Brain Sciences,* 3 (1980), 63–109. For solid and systematic naturalist accounts of belief, take a look at the works of David Armstrong, particularly his *Belief, Truth and Knowledge* (Cambridge UP, 1973), and Fred Dretske's *Knowledge and the Flow of Information* (MIT Press, 1981).

'I am getting tired. What else? *De dicto/de re?* Think of Quine, "Quantifiers and Propositional Attitudes", *Journal of Philosophy,* 53 (1956), 177–87, or Tyler Burge, "Belief De Re", *Journal of Philosophy,* 74 (1977), 338–62, or, for a deflationary (it-is-just-a-way-of-reporting-content) view, John Searle's *Intentionality* (Cambridge UP, 1983), ch. 8. The semantics of belief locutions? Start with Hintikka's *Knowledge and Belief* (Cornell UP, 1962). Unconscious belief? "Unconscious Belief" by A. Collins, *Journal of Philosophy,* 71 (1969), 667–80. Animal belief? Stich's "Do Animals Have Beliefs?", *Australasian Journal of Philosophy,* 57 (1979), 15–28. Modular belief? Stich again in "Beliefs and Subdoxastic States", *Philosophy of Science,* 45 (1978), 499–518, and, good things at the end, Fodor's *The Modularity of Mind* (MIT Press, 1983). He almost figured us out. By the way, the annoying excerpt from Lewis which I read this morning is from his paper "Mad Pain and Martian Pain" published in N. Block (ed.), *Reading in Philosophy of Psychology*, Vol. 1 (Harvard UP, 1980). Any questions?'

'Doxoi? What about the man down south you went to see at the end of your trip?'

'Oh, yes. I almost forgot. The man from New Orleans. He gave me this book with a few new articles about belief. The articles have been written for this volume and have never been published before. So take a look at them. Who knows? The man also said how grateful he was to a wonderful group of what he called "fanatic regulars", good friends and good philosophers, and how much he owed to Catalina. But don't ask me what I was doing in New Orleans, OK? And don't smile!'

CHAPTER 2

MISREPRESENTATION*

FRED DRETSKE

Epistemology is concerned with knowledge: how do we manage to get things right? There is a deeper question: how do we manage to get things wrong? How is it possible for physical systems to *misrepresent* the state of their surroundings?

The problem is not how, for example, a diagram, *d*, can misrepresent the world, *w*. For if we have another system, *r*, already possessed of representational powers, *d* can be used as an expressive extension of *r*, thereby participating in *r*'s representational successes and failures. When this occurs, *d* can come to mean that *w* is *F* when, in fact, *w* is not *F*, but *d*'s meaning derives, ultimately, from *r*. A chart depicting unemployment patterns over the past ten years can misrepresent this condition, but the chart's capacity for misrepresentation is derived from its role as an expressive instrument for agents, speakers of the language, who already have this power.

No, the problem is, rather, one of a system's powers of representation in so far as these powers do not derive from the representational efforts of another source. Unless we have some clue to how this is possible, we do not have a clue how naturally-evolving biological systems could have acquired the capacity for belief. For belief is, or so I shall assume, a *non-derived* representational capacity the exercise of which *can* yield a misrepresentation.

The capacity for misrepresentation is a part, perhaps only a small part, of the general problem of meaning or intentionality. Once we have meaning, we can, in our descriptions and explanations of human, animal, and perhaps even machine behaviour, lavish it on the systems we describe. Once we have intentionality, we can (to use Dennett's language) adopt the intentional stance.[1] But what

* © Fred Dretske 1986.
[1] D. C. Dennett, 'Intentional Systems', *Journal of Philosophy*, 68 (1971), 87–106, reprinted in *Brainstorms* (Montgomery, Vt., 1978).

(*besides* intentionality) gives us (and not, say, machines) the power to adopt this stance? Our ability to adopt this stance is an *expression*, not an analysis, of intentionality. The borrowed meaning of systems towards which we adopt appropriate attitudes tells us no more about the original capacity for misrepresentation than does a misplaced pin on a military map. What we are after, so to speak, is *nature*'s way of making a mistake, the place where the misrepresentational buck stops. Only when we understand this shall we understand how grey matter can misrepresent the weather for tomorrow's picnic.

I. NATURAL SIGNS

Naturally-occurring signs mean something, and they do so without any assistance from us.[2] Water does not flow uphill; hence, a northerly-flowing river means there is a downward gradient in that direction. Shadows to the east mean that the sun is in the west. A sudden force on the passengers in one direction means an acceleration of the train in the opposite direction. The power of these events or conditions to mean what they do is independent of the way we interpret them—or, indeed, of whether we interpret or recognize them at all. The dentist may *use* the X-ray to diagnose the condition of your upper right molar, but the dark shadows mean extensive decay has occurred whether or not he, or anyone else, appreciates this fact. Expanding metal indicates a rising temperature (and in this sense means that the temperature is rising) whether or not anyone, upon observing the former, comes to believe the latter. It meant that *before* intelligent organisms, capable of exploiting this fact (by building thermometers), inhabited the earth. If we are looking for the ultimate source of meaning, and with it an understanding of a system's power of misrepresentation, here, surely, is a promising place to begin.

  Natural signs are indicators, more or less reliable indicators, and what they mean is what they indicate to be so. The power of a natural sign to mean something—for example, that Tommy has

---

[2] This needs some qualification, but it will do for the moment. What a natural sign means often does depend on us, on what we *know* about relevant alternative possibilities or on how we *use* an associated device. But if we don't know anything, or if the sign occurs in the operation of a device having no normal use, the sign still means something—just not, specifically, what we say it means under epistemically (or functionally) richer conditions. I return to this point in n. 8 below.

measles—is underwritten by certain objective constraints, certain lawful relations, between the sign (or the sign's having a certain property) and the condition that constitutes its meaning (Tommy's having measles). In most cases this relation is causal or lawful, one capable of supporting a counterfactual assertion to the effect that if the one condition had not obtained (if Tommy did not have measles), neither would the other (he would not have those red spots all over his face). Sometimes there are merely regularities, non-lawful but none the less pervasive, that help secure the connection between sign and significance. It is partly the fact, presumably not itself lawful, that animals (for example, squirrels or woodpeckers) do not regularly ring doorbells while foraging for food that makes the ringing bell *mean* that someone (i.e. some *person*) is at the door. If squirrels changed their habits (because, say, doorbells were made out of nuts), then a ringing doorbell would no longer mean what it now does. But as things *now* stand, we can (usually) say that the bell would not be ringing unless someone was at the door, that the bell indicates someone's presence at the door, and that, therefore, that is what it means. But this subjunctively expressed dependency between the ringing bell and someone's presence at the door is a reflection of a regularity which, though not conventional, is not fully lawful either. None the less, the doorbell retains its natural meaning as long as this regularity persists.

Beyond this I have nothing very systematic to say about what constitutes the natural meaning of an event or a condition.[3] I shall proceed with what I hope is a reasonably familiar notion, appealing (when necessary) to concrete examples. The project is to see how far one can go in understanding misrepresentation, the power of a condition (state, event, situation) r to mean (say, indicate) *falsely* that w is F (thereby misrepresenting w), in terms of a natural sign's meaning that w is F. Only when (or if) this project succeeds, or shows reasonable prospects of succeeding, will it, or might it, be necessary to look more carefully at what got smuggled in at the beginning.

Though natural meaning is a promising point of departure, it is hard to see how to get under way. Natural signs, though they mean something, though they can (in this sense) represent w (by indicating or meaning that w is F) are powerless to *misrepresent* anything.

[3] I give a fuller account of it in F. Dretske, *Knowledge and the Flow of Information* (MIT Press, 1981), chs. 1 and 2.

Either they do their job right or they don't do it at all. The spots on Tommy's face certainly can mean that he has measles, but they mean this *only* when he has measles. If he doesn't have measles, then the spots don't mean this. Perhaps all they mean is that Tommy has been eating too many sweets.

Grice expresses this point by saying that an occurrence (a tokening of some natural sign) means (in what he calls the natural sense of 'meaning'—hereafter meaning$_n$) that P only if P.[4] He contrasts this sense of meaning with non-natural meaning where a sign can mean that P even though P is false. If we reserve the word 'meaning' (minus subscripts) for that species of meaning in which something can mean that w is F when w isn't F, the kind of meaning in which misrepresentation is possible, then meaning$_n$ seems a poorly-qualified candidate for understanding meaning.

In speaking of signs and their natural meaning I should always be understood as referring to *particular* events, states or conditions: *this* track, *those* clouds, and *that* smoke. A sign type (for example, smoke) may be said to mean, in some natural sense, that there is fire even when every token of that type fails to mean$_n$ this (because, occasionally, there is no fire). But this type-associated meaning, whatever its proper analysis, does *not* help us understand misrepresentation unless the individual tokens of that type *have* the type-associated meaning, unless particular puffs of smoke mean$_n$ that there is fire when there is no fire. This, though, is not the case. A petrol gauge's registration of 'empty' (this *type* of event) can signify an empty tank, but when the tank is not empty, no particular registration of 'empty' by the gauge's pointer means$_n$ that the tank is empty. Hence, no particular registration of the gauge misrepresents the amount of gas in the tank (by meaning$_n$ that it is empty when it is not).

The inability of (particular) natural signs to misrepresent anything is sometimes obscured by the way we exploit them in manufactured devices. Interested as we may be in whether, and if so when, w becomes F, we concoct a device d whose various states are designed to function as natural signs of w's condition. Since this is how we use the device, we tend to say of some particular registration that d's being G (assuming this is the natural sign of w's being F) means that w is F even when, through malfunction or misuse, the system is

[4] P. Grice, 'Meaning', *Philosophical Review*, 66 (1957), 377–88.

failing to perform satisfactorily and w is not F. But this, clearly, is not what the particular pointer position means$_n$. This is what it is *supposed* to mean$_n$, what it was *designed* to mean$_n$, what (perhaps) tokens of type *normally* mean$_n$, but not what it *does* mean$_n$.

When there is a short circuit, the ring of the doorbell (regardless of what it was designed to indicate, regardless of what it normally indicates) does not indicate that the bellpush is being pressed. It still means$_n$ (indicates) that there is electric current flowing in the doorbell circuit (one of the things it always meant$_n$), but the latter no longer means$_n$ that the bellpush is being pressed. What the flow of current *now* means$_n$—and this is surely how we would judge it if we could *see* the bellpush, *see that* it was *not* being pressed—is that the system is malfunctioning or that there is a short circuit somewhere in the wiring. The *statement*, 'There is someone at the door', can mean that there is someone at the door even when no one is there, but the ringing doorbell cannot mean this when no one is there. Not, at least, if we are talking about meaning$_n$. If the bellpush is not being pressed, then we must look for something else for the ringing bell to mean$_n$. Often, we withdraw to some more proximal meaning$_n$, some condition or state of affairs in the normal chain of causal antecedents that *does* obtain (for example, the flow of current or the *cause* of the flow of current—for example, a short circuit) and designate it as the meaning$_n$ of the ringing bell.

2. FUNCTIONAL MEANING

Granted, one may say, the doorbell's ringing cannot mean$_n$ that someone is at the door when no one is there; still, in some related sense of meaning, it means this whether or not anyone is there. If this is not natural meaning (meaning$_n$), it is a close cousin.

Whether it is a cousin or not, there certainly is a kind of meaning that attaches to systems, or components of systems, for which there are identifiable *functions*. Consider, once again, the fuel gauge. It has a function: to pass along information about the amount of petrol in the tank. When things are working properly, the position of the needle is a natural sign of the contents of the tank. Its pointing to the left means$_n$ that the tank is empty. Its pointing to the right means$_n$ that the tank is full. And so on for the intermediate positions. But things sometimes go wrong: connections work loose, the battery goes dead, wires break. The gauge begins to register 'empty' when the tank is still full. When this happens there is a tendency to say that the gauge misrepresents the contents of the tank. It *says* the tank is empty when it is not. It *means* (not, of course, means$_n$), but still means in *some* sense) that the tank is empty.

When d's being G is, normally, a natural sign of w's being F, when this is what it normally means$_n$, then there is a sense in which it means this whether or not w is F *if it is the function of d to indicate the condition of w*. Let us call this kind of meaning *meaning$_f$*—the subscript indicating that this is a functionally derived meaning.

> (M_f) d's being G means$_f$ that w is $F = d$'s function is to indicate the condition of w, and the way it performs this function is, in part, by indicating that w is F by its (d's) being G

The position of the needle on the broken fuel gauge means$_f$ that the tank is empty because it is the gauge's function to indicate the amount of remaining fuel, and the way it performs this function is, in part, by indicating an empty tank when the gauge registers 'empty'.[5] And, for the same reason and in the same sense, the ringing doorbell says (i.e. means$_f$) that someone is at the door even when no one is there.

Whether or not M_f represents any progress in our attempt to naturalize meaning (and thus understand a system's non derivative power to misrepresent) depends on whether the functions in question can themselves be understood in some natural way. If these functions are (what I shall call) *assigned* functions, then meaning$_f$ is tainted with the purposes, intentions, and beliefs of those who assign the function from which meaning$_f$ derives its misrepresentational powers.[6] We shall not have tracked meaning, in so far as this involves the power of misrepresentation, to its original source. We shall merely have worked our way back, somewhat indirectly, to *our own* mysterious capacity for representation.

To understand what I mean by an *assigned* function, and the way

---

[5] I hope it is clear, that I am not here concerned with the word 'empty' (or the letter 'E') that might appear on the gauge. This symbol means empty whatever the gauge is doing, but this is purely conventional. I am concerned with what the pointer's position means$_n$ *whatever* we choose to print on the face of the instrument.

[6] L. Wright calls these 'conscious' functions; see his 'Functions', *Philosophical Review*, 82.2 (Apr. 1973), 142.

we (our intentions, purposes and beliefs) are implicated in a system's having such a function, consider the following case. A sensitive spring-operated scale, calibrated in fractions of a gram, is designed and used to determine the weight of very small objects. Unknown to both designers and users, the instrument is a sensitive indicator of altitude. By registering a reduced weight for things as altitude increases (note: a things weight is a function of its height above sea level), the instrument *could* be used as a crude altimeter if the user attached a standard weight and noted the instrument's variable registration as altitude changed. Suppose, now, that under normal use in the laboratory the instrument malfunctions and registers 0.98 g. for an object weighing 1 g. Is it misrepresenting the *weight* of the object? Is it misrepresenting the *altitude* of the object? What does the reading of 0.98 g. mean? If we are talking about meaning$_n$, it clearly does not mean$_n$ that the object weighs 0.98 g. Nor does it mean$_n$ that the laboratory is 40,000 ft. above sea level. If we ask about meaning$_f$, though, it seems reasonable to say that the instrument's pointer says or indicates (i.e. means$_f$) that the object weighs 0.98 g. It is the function of this instrument to tell us what objects weigh, and it is telling us (incorrectly, as it turns out) that this object weighs 0.98 g.

But is the altitude being misrepresented? No. It should be noticed that the instrument cannot be misrepresenting *both* the altitude and the weight since a representation (or misrepresentation) of one presupposes a *fixity* (hence, *non*-representation) of the other.[7] Although the instrument *could* be used as an altimeter, it *is not* used that way. That is not its function. Its function is to register weight. That is the function we assign to it, the reason it was built and the explanation why it was built the way it was. Had our purposes been otherwise, it might have meant$_f$ something else. But they were not and it does not.

We sometimes change an instrument's assigned function. When we calibrate it, for example, we do not use it to measure what it is normally used to measure. Instead, we apply it to known quantities in order to use its indication as a (natural) sign of possible malfunction or inaccuracy in the instrument itself. In this case, a reading of 0.98 g. (for a weight *known* to be 1 g.) indicates that the spring has changed its characteristics, the pointer is bent, or some other

---

[7] A doorbell, for example, cannot mean$_n$ *both* that there is someone at the door *and* that there is a short circuit.

component is out of adjustment. We get a new functional meaning because our altered background knowledge (normally a result of different intentions and purposes) changes what the pointer's behaviour means$_n$. With *assigned* functions, the meanings$_f$ change as *our* purposes change.[8]

We sometimes use animals in the same way that we use instruments. Dogs have an acute sense of smell. Exploiting this fact, customs officers use dogs to detect concealed marijuana. When the dog wags its tail, barks, or does whatever it is trained to do when it smells marijuana, the dog's behaviour serves as a natural sign—a sign that the luggage contains marijuana. But this does not mean that the dog's behaviour (or the neural condition that triggers this behaviour) can misrepresent the contents of the luggage. The dog's behaviour may make the customs officer believe (falsely) that there is marijuana in the suitcase, but the dog's behaviour means$_f$ this only in a derived way. If the dog is particularly good at its job, barking only when there is marijuana present, we can say that its bark indicates (i.e. means$_n$) that there is marijuana present. Furthermore, it means$_n$ this whether or not anyone interprets it as meaning$_n$ this, whether or not we *use* this natural sign for our own investigative purposes. But when there is no marijuana present, when the dog barks at an innocent box of herbs, the bark does *not* mean$_n$ that there is marijuana present. Nor does it mean$_f$ this in any sense that is independent of *our* interpretative activities. We can, of course, say what the bark means *to us* (that there is marijuana in the suitcase), but this way of talking merely reveals our own involvement in the meaning assigned to the dog's behaviour. *We* assign this meaning because this is the information we are *interested* in obtaining, the information we *expect* to get by using the dog in this way, the information the dog was trained to deliver. But if we set aside our interests and purposes, then, *when there is no marijuana present*, there is *no* sense in which the dog's bark means that there is

---

[8] It isn't the change of purpose *alone* that changes what something means$_n$ (hence, means$_f$). It is the fact that this change in use is accompanied by altered background knowledge, and meaning$_n$ changes as background knowledge changes. If, for example, A depends on both B and C, a changing A can mean$_n$ that C is changing *if* we know that B is constant. If we know that C is constant, it can mean$_n$ that B is changing. If we know nothing, it only means that either B or C is changing. Natural meaning is relative in this sense, but derelativizing it (by ignoring what we know and how we use a device) does not eliminate natural meaning. It merely makes *less determinate* what things mean$_n$. For a fuller discussion of this point, see ch. 3 in Dretske, *Knowledge and the Flow of Information*.

marijuana in the suitcase. The only kind of misrepresentation occurring here is of the derived kind we are familiar with in maps, instruments, and language.

Therefore, if M_f is to serve as a naturalized account of representation, where this is understood to include the power of *mis*-representation, then the functions in question must be *natural* functions, functions a thing has which are independent of *our* interpretative intentions and purposes. What we are looking for are functions involving a system of natural signs that give these signs a content, and therefore a meaning (i.e. a meaning$_f$), that is not parasitic on the way *we* exploit them in our information-gathering activities, on the way we choose to interpret them.[9]

We need, then, some characterization of a system's natural functions. More particularly, since we are concerned with the function a system of natural signs might have, we are looking for what a sign is *supposed* to mean$_n$ where the 'supposed to' is cashed out in terms of the function of that sign (or sign system) in the organism's *own* cognitive economy. We want to know how *the dog* represents the contents of the luggage—what (if anything) the smell of the box means$_f$ *to it*.

3. NEEDS

The obvious place to look for natural functions is in biological systems having a variety of organs, mechanisms, and processes that were developed (flourished, preserved) *because* they played a vital information-gathering role in the species' adaptation to its surroundings. An information-gathering function, essential in most cases to the satisfaction of a biological need, can only be successfully realized in a system capable of occupying states that serve as natural signs of external (and sometimes *other* internal) conditions. If that cluster of photoreceptors we call the retina is to perform its function (whatever, exactly, we take this function to be), the various states of these receptors must mean$_n$ something about the character and distribution of one's optical surroundings. Just what the various

---

[9] I think much of our talk about the representational capacities of computers is of this assigned, hence derived, kind. It tells us nothing about the intrinsic power of a machine to represent or misrepresent anything. Hence, nothing about the cognitive character of its internal states. R. Cummins, I think, gets it exactly right by distinguishing *cognition (a version of *assigned* meaning) from genuine cognition. See his *Psychological Explanation* (MIT Press, 1983).

states these receptors mean$_f$ will (in accordance with M_f) be determined by two things: (1) what it is the function of this receptor system to indicate, and (2) the meaning$_n$ of the various states that enable the system to perform this function.

To illustrate the way M_f is supposed to work it is convenient to consider simple organisms with obvious biological needs—some thing or condition without which they could not survive. I say this is convenient because this approach to the problem of misrepresentation has its most compelling application to cognitive mechanisms subserving some basic biological need. And the consideration of *primitive* systems gives us the added advantage of avoiding that kind of circularity in the analysis that would be incurred by appealing to those kinds of 'needs' (for example, my need for a word processor) that are derived from desires (for example, my desire to produce faster, cleaner copy). We cannot bring desires in at this stage of the analysis since they already possess the kind of representational content that we are trying to understand.

Some marine bacteria have internal magnets (called magnetosomes) that function like compass needles, aligning themselves (and, as a result, the bacteria) parallel to the earth's magnetic field.[10] Since these magnetic lines incline downwards (towards geomagnetic north) in the northern hemisphere (upwards in the southern hemisphere), bacteria in the northern hemisphere, oriented by their internal magnetosomes, propel themselves towards geomagnetic north. The survival value of magnetotaxis (as this sensory mechanism is called) is not obvious, but it is reasonable to suppose that it functions so as to enable the bacteria to avoid surface water. Since these organisms are capable of living only in the absence of oxygen, movement towards geomagnetic north will take the bacteria away from oxygen-rich surface water and towards the comparatively oxygen-free sediment at the bottom. Southern-hemispheric bacteria have their magnetosomes reversed, allowing them to swim towards geomagnetic south with the same beneficial results. Transplant a southern bacterium in the North Atlantic and it will destroy itself—swimming upwards (towards magnetic south) into the toxic, oxygen-rich surface water.

If a bar magnet oriented in the opposite direction to the earth's magnetic field is held near these bacteria, they can be lured into a

[10] My source for this example is R. P. Blakemore and R. B. Frankel, 'Magnetic Navigation in Bacteria', *Scientific American*, 245. 6 (Dec. 1981).

deadly environment. Although I shall return to the point in a moment (in order to question this line of reasoning), this appears to be a plausible instance of misrepresentation. Since, in the bacteria's normal habitat, the internal orientation of their magnetosomes means$_n$ that there is relatively little oxygen in *that* direction, and since the organism needs precisely this piece of information in order to survive, it seems reasonable to say that it is the function of this sensory mechanism to serve the satisfaction of this need, to deliver this piece of information, to indicate that oxygen-free water is in *that* direction. If this is what it is *supposed* to mean$_n$, this is what it means$_f$. Hence, in the presence of the bar magnet and in accordance with M_f, the organism's sensory state misrepresents the location of oxygen-free water.

This is not to say, of course, that bacteria have *beliefs*, beliefs to the effect that there is little or no oxygen in *that* direction. The capacity for misrepresentation is only *one* dimension of intentionality, only *one* of the properties that a representational system must have to qualify as a belief system. To qualify as a belief, a representational content must also exhibit (among other things) the familiar opacity characteristic of the propositional attitudes, and, unless embellished in some way, meaning$_f$ does not (yet) exhibit *this* level of intentionality. Our project, though, is more modest. We are looking for a naturalized form of misrepresentation and, if we do not yet have an account of false *belief*, we do, it seems, have a naturalized account of false *content*.

Apart from some terminological flourishes and a somewhat different way of structuring the problem, nothing I have said so far is particularly original. I have merely been retracing steps, some very significant steps, already taken by others. I am thinking especially of Stampe's seminal analysis of linguistic representation in which the (possibly false) content of a representation is identified with what would cause the representation to have the properties it has under conditions of well-functioning[11]; Enc's development of functional ideas to provide an account of the intentionality of cognitive states[12]; Fodor's application of teleological notions in

[11] D. Stampe, 'Toward a Causal Theory of Linguistic Representation', in P. French, T. Uehling, and H. Wettstein (edd.), *Midwest Studies in Philosophy*, Vol. 2 (University of Minnesota Press, 1977).

[12] B. Enc, 'Intentional States of Mechanical Devices', *Mind*, 91 (Apr. 1982), 362. Enc identified the content of a functional state with the (construction of the) properties of the event to which the system has the function of responding.

supplying a semantics for his 'language of thought'[13]; and Millikan's powerful analysis of meaning in terms of the variety of proper functions a reproducible event (such as a sound or a gesture) might have.[14] I myself have tried to exploit (vaguely) functional ideas in my analysis of belief by defining a structure's semantic content in terms of the information it was developed to carry (hence, acquired the function of carrying).[15]

4. THE INDETERMINACY OF FUNCTION

Though this approach to the problem of meaning—and, hence, misrepresentation—has been explored in some depth, there remain obstacles to regarding it as even a promising sketch, let alone a finished portrait, of nature's way of making a mistake.

There is, first, the question of how to understand a system's ability to misrepresent something for which it has no biological need. If O does not need (or need to avoid) F, it cannot (on the present account) be the *natural* function of any of O's cognitive systems to alert it to the presence (absence, location, approach, identity) of F. And without this, there is no possibility of *mis*-representing something *as F*. Some internal state could still mean$_n$ that an F was present (in the way the state of Rover's detector system means$_n$ that the luggage contains marijuana), but this internal state cannot *mean$_f$* this. What we have so far is a way of understanding how an organism might misrepresent the presence of food, an obstacle, a predator, or a mate (something there is a biological need to secure or avoid[16]), but no way of understanding how *we* can misrepresent things as, say, can-openers, tennis-rackets, tulips, or the jack of diamonds. Even if we suppose our nervous systems sophisticated enough to indicate (under normal conditions) the presence of such things, it surely cannot be the *natural* function of these neural states to signal the presence—much less, specific kinds—of kitchen utensils, sporting equipment, flowers, and playing cards.

[13] J. Fodor, 'Psychosemantics, or Where Do Truth Conditions Come From?' *manuscript*.

[14] R, Millikan, *Language, Thought and other Biological Categories* (MIT Press, 1984).

[15] Dretske, *Knowledge and the Flow of Information*, part 3.

[16] Something for which there is, in Dennett's (earlier) language, an 'appropriate efferent continuation': see his *Content and Consciousness* (London, 1969).

I think this is a formidable, but *not* an insuperable, difficulty. For it seems clear that a cognitive system might develop so as to service, and hence have the natural function of servicing, some biological need without its representational (*and* misrepresentational) efforts being confined to these needs. In order to identify its natural predator, an organism might develop detectors of colour, shape, and movement of considerable discriminative power. Equipped, then, with this capacity for differentiating various colours, shapes, and movements, the organism acquires, as a fringe benefit so to speak, the ability to identify (and, hence, misidentify) things for which it has no biological need. The creature may have no need for green leaves, but its need for pink blossoms has led to the development of a cognitive system whose various states are capable, because of their need-related meaning$_f$, to mean$_f$ that there are green leaves present. Perhaps, though having no need for such things, it has developed a taste for them and hence a way of representing them with elements that already have a meaning$_f$.

There is, however, a more serious objection to this approach to the problem of misrepresentation. Consider, once again, the bacteria. It was said that it was the function of their magnetotactic system to indicate the whereabouts of oxygen-free environments. But why describe the function of this system in this way? Why not say that it is the function of this system to indicate the direction of geomagnetic north? Perhaps, to be even more modest, we should assign to this sensor the function of indicating the whereabouts (direction) of magnetic (not necessarily *geo*magnetic) north. This primitive sensory mechanism is, after all, functioning perfectly well when, under the bar magnet's influence, it leads its possessor into a toxic environment. *Something* is going wrong in this case, of course, but I see no reason to place the blame on the sensory mechanism, no reason to say it is not performing *its* function. One may as well complain that a fuel gauge is not performing its function when the petrol tank is filled with water (and the driver is consequently misled about the amount of *petrol* he has left). Under such abnormal circumstances, the instrument is performing its duties in a perfectly satisfactory way—i.e., indicating the amount of liquid in the tank. What has gone wrong is something for which the instrument itself is not responsible: namely, a breakdown in the normal correlations (between the quantity of liquid in the tank and the quantity of petrol in the tank) that make the gauge serviceable as a *fuel* gauge, that allow it (when conditions are normal) to mean$_n$ that there is petrol in the tank. Similarly, there is nothing wrong with one's perceptual system when one consults a slow-running clock and is, as a result, misled about the time of day. It is the function of one's eyes to tell one what *the clock says*; it is the function of *the clock to* say what the time is. Getting things right about what you need to know is often a *shared* responsibility. You have to get *G* right and *G* has to get *F* right. Hence, even if it is *F* that you need, or need to know about, the function of the perceptual system may be only to inform you of *G*.

If we think about the bacterium's sensory system in this way, then *its* function is to align the organism with the prevailing magnetic field. It is, so to speak, the job of magnetic north to be the direction of oxygen-free water. By transplanting a northern bacterium in the southern hemisphere we can make things go awry, but *not* because a hemispheric transplant undergoes *sensory* disorientation. No, the magnetotactic system functions as it is supposed to function, as it was (presumably) evolved to function. The most that might be claimed is that there is some *cognitive* slip (the bacterium mistakenly 'infers' from its sensory condition that *that* is the direction of oxygen-free water). This sort of reply, however, begs the question by presupposing that the creature *already* has the conceptual or representational capacity to represent something *as* the direction of oxygen-free water. Our question is *whether* the organism has this capacity and, if so, where it comes from.[17]

Northern bacteria, it is true, have no need to live in northerly climes *qua* northerly climes. So to describe the function of the bacterium's detectors in terms of the role they play in identifying geomagnetic north is not to describe them in ways that reveal *how*

[17] Fodor (in a circulated draft of 'Why Paramecia Don't Have Mental Representations') distinguishes organisms for which a representational theory of mind is not appropriate (paramecia, for example) and ones for which it is (us, for example) in terms of the latter's ability to respond to non-nomic stimulus properties (properties that are not transducer-detectable). We, but not paramecia, are capable of representing something as, say, a crumpled shirt, and *being a crumpled shirt* is not a projectible property. In this article, Fodor is not concerned with the question of *where* we get this extraordinary representational power from (he suggests it requires inferential capacities). He is concerned only with offering it as a way of distinguishing us from a variety of other perceptual and quasi-cognitive systems.

I agree with Fodor about the importance and relevance of this distinction, but my present concern is to understand *how* a system could acquire the power to represent something in this way. The power to represent something *as* a crumpled shirt (where this implies the correlative ability to misrepresent it as such) is certainly not innate.

this function is related to the satisfaction of its needs. But we do not have to describe the function of a mechanism in terms of its possessor's ultimate biological needs.[18] It is the function of the heart to circulate the blood. Just *why* the blood needs to be circulated may be a mystery.

So the sticky question is: *given* that a system needs F, and *given* that mechanism M enables the organism to detect, identify or recognize F, *how* does the mechanism carry out this function? Does it do so by representing nearby Fs *as nearby Fs* or does it, perhaps, represent them merely *as nearby Gs*, trusting to nature (the correlation between F and G) for the satisfaction of its needs? To describe a cognitive mechanism as an F-detector (and, therefore, as a mechanism that plays a vital role in the satisfaction of an organism's needs) is not *yet* to tell the functional story by means of which this mechanism does its job. All we know when we know that O needs F and that m enables O to detect F is that M *either* means$_f$ that F is prsent *or* it means$_f$ that G is present where G is, in O's natural surroundings, a natural sign of F's presence (where G means$_n$ F).[19] If I need vitamin C, my perceptual–cognitive system should not automatically be credited with the capacity for recognizing objects *as* containing vitamin C (as meaning$_f$ that they contain vitamin C) just because it supplies me with the information required to satisfy

[18] Enc, 'Intentional States of Mechanical Devices', p. 168, says that a photoreceptor in the fruit-fly has the function of enabling the fly to reach humid spots (in virtue of the correlation between dark spots and humid spots). I have no objection to describing things in this way. But the question remains: *how* does it perform this function? We can answer this question without supposing that there is any mechanism of the fly whose function it is to indicate the degree of humidity. The sensory mechanism can perform this function if there is merely something to indicate the luminosity—i.e. a photoreceptor. *That* will enable the fly to reach humid spots. Likewise, the bacteria's magnetotactic sense *enables* (and, let us say, has the *function* of enabling) the bacteria to avoid oxygen-rich water. But the way it does it (it may be argued) is by having a sensor that indicates, and has the function of indicating, the direction of the magnetic field.

[19] In Fodor's way of putting the point (in 'Psychosemantics'), this is merely a way of saying that his identification of the semantics of M (some mental representation) with entry conditions (relative to a set of normalcy conditions) still leaves some slack. We can say that the entry condition is the absence (presence) of oxygen *or* a specific orientation of the magnetic field. Appeal to the selectional history of this mechanism won't decide *which* is the right specification of entry conditions—hence, won't tell us whether the bacteria are capable of *mis*representing anything. Fodor, I think, realizes this residual indeterminacy and makes the suggestive remark (n. 9) that this problem is an analogue of the problems of specifying the perceptual object for theories of perception.

this need. Representing things as oranges and lemons will do quite nicely.

The problem we face is the problem of accounting for the misrepresentational capacities of a system *without* doing so by artificially *inflating* the natural functions of such a system. We need some *principled* way of saying what the natural function of a mechanism is, what its various states not only mean$_n$, but what they *mean*$_f$. It sounds a bit far-fetched (to my ear at least) to describe the bacteria's sensory mechanism as indicating, and having the function of indicating, the whereabouts of oxygen. For this makes it sound as though it is not performing its function under deceptive conditions (for example, in the presence of a bar magnet). This is, after all, a *magneto*tactic, not a *chemo*tactic, sensor. But if we choose to describe the function of this sensor in this more modest way, we no longer have an example of a system with misrepresentational powers. A northern bacterium (transplanted in the southern hemisphere) will not be misrepresenting anything when, under the guidance of its magnetotactic sensor, it moves upwards (towards geomagnetic north) into the lethal surface water. The alignment of its magnetosomes will mean$_n$ what it has always meant$_n$, what it is its function to mean$_n$, what it is supposed to mean$_n$: namely, that *that* is the direction of magnetic north. The disaster can be blamed on the abnormal surroundings. Nor can we salvage some residual misrepresentational capacity by supposing that the bacterium, under the influence of a bar magnet, at least misrepresents the direction of geomagnetic north. For, once again, the same problem emerges: why suppose it is the function of this mechanism to indicate the direction of *geo*magnetic north rather than, simply, the direction of the surrounding magnetic field? If we describe the function only in the latter way, it becomes impossible to fool the organism, impossible to make it misrepresent anything. For its internal states only mean$_f$ that the magnetic field is pointing in *that* direction and (like a compass) this is always accurate.

5. FUNCTIONAL DETERMINATION

For the purpose of clarifying issues, I have confined the discussion to simple organisms with primitive representational capacities. It is not surprising, then, to find no clear and unambiguous capacity for misrepresentation at this level. For this power—and, presumably, the dependent capacity for belief—requires a certain threshold of complexity in the information-processing capabilities of a system. Somewhere between the single cell and man we cross that threshold. It is the purpose of this final section to describe the character of this threshold, to describe the *kind* of complexity responsible for the misrepresentational capabilities of higher organisms.

Suppose an organism (unlike our bacterium) has *two* ways of detecting the presence of some toxic substance F. This may be because the organism is equipped with two sense modalities, each (in their different way) sensitive to F (or some modally specific natural sign of F), or because a single sense modality exploits different external signs (or symptoms) of F. As an example of the latter, consider the way we might identify oak trees visually by either one of two ways: by the distinctive leaf pattern (in the summer) or by the characteristic texture and pattern of the bark (in winter). We have, then, two internal states or conditions, I_1 and I_2, each produced by a different chain of antecedent events, that are natural signs of the presence of F. Each means$_n$ that F is present. Suppose, furthermore, that, having a need to escape from the toxic F, these internal states are harnessed to a third state, call it R, which triggers or releases a pattern of avoidance behaviour. Figure 2 assembles the relevant facts. R, of course, is also a natural sign of F. Under normal circumstances, R does not occur unless F is present. f_1 and f_2 are properties typical of normal Fs. s_1 and s_2 are proximal stimuli.

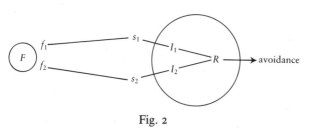

Fig. 2

If, now, we present the system with some ersatz F (analogous to the bar magnet with the bacteria), something exhibiting *some* of the properties of the real f (say f_1), we trigger a chain of events (s_1, I_1, R and avoidance) that normally occurs, and is really only appropriate, in the presence of F. If we look at the internal state R and ask what it means$_f$ under these deceptive conditions, we find ourselves unable to say (as we could in the case of the bacteria) that it means$_f$ anything short of (i.e. more proximal than) F itself. Even though s_1 (by means of I_1) is triggering the occurrence of R, R does not mean$_n$ (hence, cannot mean$_f$) that s_1 (or f_1) is occurring. R is analogous to a light bulb connected to switches wired in parallel *either* of whose closure will turn the light on. When the bulb lights up, it does not mean$_n$ that switch no. 1 is closed even when it is this switch's closure that causes the light to go on. It does not mean$_n$ this, because there is no regular correlation between the bulb lighting up and switch no. 1 being closed (50 per cent of the time it it switch no. 2).

If we think of the detection system described above as having the function of enabling the organism to detect F, then the multiplicity of ways of detecting F has the consequence that certain internal states (for example, R) can indicate (hence mean$_f$) that F is present without indicating anything about the intermediate conditions (i.e. f_1 or s_1) that 'tell' it that F is present. Our problem with the bacteria was to find a way of having the orientation of its magnetosomes mean$_f$ that oxygen-free water was in a certain direction without *arbitrarily* dismissing the possibility of its meaning$_f$ that the magnetic field was aligned in that direction. We can now see that, with the multiple resources described in Figure 2, this possibility can be *non*-arbitrarily dismissed. R *cannot* mean$_f$ that f_1 or s_1 is occurring, because it *does not*, even under optimal conditions, mean$_n$ this. We can therefore claim to have found a non-derivative case of misrepresentation (i.e., R's meaning$_f$ that F is present when it is not) which cannot be dismissed by redescribing what R means$_f$ so as to eliminate the appearance of misrepresentation. The threatened inflation of possible meanings$_f$, arising from the variety of ways a system's natural function might be described, has been blocked.

Still, it will be said, we *need not* accept this as a case of genuine misrepresentation *if* we are prepared to recognize that R has a *disjunctive* meaning$_n$. The lighting up of the bulb (connected to switches wired in parallel) does not mean$_n$ that any particular switch is on, but it does indicate that *one* of the switches is on. Similarly, it may be said, even though it is the function of the mechanism having R as its terminal state to alert the organism to the presence of F, it does so by R's indicating, and having the function of indicating, the occurrence of a certain disjunctive condition—namely, that either f_1 or f_2 (or s_1 or s_2). Our hypothetical organism mistakenly withdraws from F, *not* because it misrepresents the ersatz F as F, but because what it correctly indicates (i.e. that the ersatz f is either f_1 or f_2) is no longer correlated in the normal way with something's being F.

No matter how versatile a detection system we might design, no matter how many routes of informational access we might give an organism, the possibility will always exist of describing its function (and therefore the meaning$_f$ of its various states) as the detection of some highly disjunctive property of the proximal input. At least, this will always be possible *if* we have a determinate set of disjuncts to which we can retreat.

Suppose, however, that we have a system capable of some form of associative learning. Suppose, in other words, that through repeated exposures to *cs* (a conditioned stimulus) in the presence of F, a change takes place. R (and, hence, avoidance behaviour) can now be triggered by the occurrence of *cs* alone. Furthermore, it becomes clear that there is virtually no limit to the kind of stimulus that can acquire this 'displaced' effectiveness in triggering R and subsequent avoidance behaviour. Almost any s can become a *cs*, thereby assuming 'control' over R, by functioning (in the 'experience' of the organism) as a sign of F.

We now have a cognitive mechanism that not only transforms a variety of different sensory inputs (the s_i) into *one* output-determining state (R), but is capable of modifying the character of this many–one mapping over time. If we restrict ourselves to the sensory inputs (the s_i of Figure 2), R means$_n$ one thing at t_1 (for example, that either s_1 or s_2), something else at t_2 (for example, that either s_1 or s_2 or, through learning, cs_3), and something still different at a later time. Just *what* R means$_n$ will depend on the individual's learning history—on *what* s_i became cs_i *for it*. There is no *time-invariant* meaning$_n$ for R; hence, nothing that, through time, could be its function to indicate. In terms of the s_i that produce R, R can have no time-invariant meaning$_f$.

Of course, throughout this process, R continues to indicate the presence of F. It does so because, by hypothesis, any new s_i to which R becomes conditioned is a natural sign of F. Learning is a process in which stimuli that indicate the presence of F are, in their turn, indicated by some relevant internal state of the organism (R in this case). Therefore, if we are to think of these cognitive mechanisms as having a time-invariant function at all (something that is implied by their continued—indeed, as a result of learning, more efficient—servicing of the associated need), then we *must* think of their function, not as indicating the nature of the proximal (even distal) conditions that trigger positive responses (the s_i and f_1), but as indicating the condition (F) for which these diverse stimuli are signs. The mechanism just described has, then, as its natural function, the indication of the presence of F. Hence, the occurrence of R means$_f$ that F is present. It does not mean$_f$ that s_1 or s_2 or . . . s_x obtains, even though, at any given stage of development, it will mean$_n$ this for some definite value of x.

A system at this level of complexity, having not only multiple channels of access to what it needs to know about, but the resources for expanding its information-gathering resources, possesses, I submit, a genuine power of misrepresentation. When there is a breakdown in the normal chain of natural signs, when, say, cs_7 occurs (a learned sign of F) under circumstances in which it does not mean$_n$ that F is present (in the way that the broken clock does not mean$_n$ that it is 3.30 a.m.), R still means$_f$ (though not, of course, means$_n$) that F is present. It means$_f$ this because that is what it is *supposed* to mean$_n$, what it is its natural function to mean$_n$, and there is available no other condition it can mean$_f$.[20]

[20] I am grateful to Berent Enc, Dennis Stampe, and Jerry Fodor for their helpful criticisms, both constructive and destructive, of earlier drafts of this essay.

CHAPTER 3

METAMIND: BELIEF, CONSCIOUSNESS, AND INTENTIONALITY*

KEITH LEHRER

Thomas Reid articulated a theory of conception and belief that was a significant contribution in his day and which has contemporary relevance.[1] My interest in Reid in this paper is not primarily historical. I wish to build on and develop the sort of theory of conception and belief that Reid defended. I use Reid's presentation as an expositional strategy. I believe, of course, that Reid held the doctrines I attribute to him, but it is the truth of those doctrines rather than their attribution to Reid that concerns me here. My only fundamental disagreement with Reid concerns his dualism. That I reject at the end of the paper.

Reid gives a central role to intentionality and consciousness. He maintains that conception and belief presuppose an operation of the mind that is innate, part of our natural constitution, and interprets the original signs of sense. Reid's theory of belief is based on his theory of conception and meaning. This theory incorporates the division-of-labour theory of meaning. Reid anticipated modern theories of meaning, conception, and belief, especially causal theories, but his understanding of the role of consciousness in conception and belief renders his theory distinct from his modern rivals. He discovered that ordinary conception and belief presuppose consciousness of our mental activity, and, therefore, that the human mind is essentially a metamind.

* © Keith Lehrer 1986.
[1] My account of Reid is based on his books *An Inquiry into the Human Mind on the Principles of Common Sense* (Edinburgh, 1764) and *Essays on the Intellectual Powers of Man* (Edinburgh, 1785). The most readily available edition of Reid is R. Beanblossom and K. Lehrer (edd.), *Thomas Reid's Inquiry and Essays* (New York, 1984), and page references are to this edition.

Acts of belief

Reid distinguished between the operation of believing, the mental act, and the object of belief, the content. The act of believing is, Reid avers, simple and unanalysable. He also says that believing something to be the case and judging it to be the case are one and the same. It is a fundamental feature of Reid's theory that neither believing nor judging need be remembered. When we experience sensations, for example, they are signs that occasion a conception and belief of their existence as well as of external qualities and objects. Though we believe the sensations exist, we may immediately forget them when they are of no particular interest. Reid, being a rather keen observer, had noted short-term memory. He distinguished between physical impressions on the organs of sense and sensations in the mind. Reid recognized the importance of distinguishing between those physical processes which, though they are a necessary condition of perception and thought, are not conceived and other processes which are. The former he thought of as physical processes of the body and the latter as operations of the mind. Reid was, of course, a dualist. Sensations are conceived, we have a conception of them, but we do not attend to the sensations unless they are particularly salient. Hence, our conception and belief of the existence of many sensations is immediately forgotten.

Another example of immediately forgotten belief would be the remarks of someone which you listen to but do not find the least bit interesting. You immediately forget what the person says, upon hearing him. The speaker, though boring, may be quite trustworthy, however. You may believe what he says, even though you do not subsequently remember it at all. Reading something boring would be another example. You may believe but not remember what you read. Some signs, whether sensations, speech, or printed letters, are automatically understood and assumed to be truthful but forgotten. We can train ourselves to attend to and remember some of these things if we wish, but ordinarily they are not remembered. This is why Reid thought that the act of belief was not analysable as a long-term disposition to think, speak, or otherwise behave in any specified manner. A belief may last no longer than the understanding of a sign.

The importance of such a claim for a theory of belief is largely negative. It serves to preclude theories of belief that attempt to analyse belief in terms of some long-term disposition to act or even to fulfil any functional role that assumes the retention of the belief. Acts of belief are not dispositional states. They are occurrent mental operations, and they are known immediately. To argue to the contrary, as Reid insisted, is to argue for a hypothesis against the facts. Reid is thus opposed to a dispositional theory of belief according to which beliefs are known through their effects. Thus, he would be opposed to such modern theorists as Barwise and Perry, who remark, 'Beliefs are dispositional states; that is, real states known through their effects'.[2] This is not to deny that beliefs have effects, of course, since occurrent states have effects. These occurrent states may, moreover, give rise to dispositional states as a result of being stored in memory. To equate the beliefs with the dispositions to which they give rise is, however, an error.

Objects of belief

Reid says that there is no belief without conception. For something to be an object of belief, you must have a conception of it. The object of conception is the object of belief. Conception is itself an activity of the mind, a simple and unanalysable operation. When we speak of conceptions and beliefs, there is a certain ambiguity that Reid noted. We use these terms sometimes to refer to the mental operation or activity and sometimes to the object or content of that activity. He suggests that this ambiguity leads to the philosophical error of supposing that the object of conception and belief is always something mental. The theory that the object of thought is always something mental, an idea or impression, as Hume alleged, is the result of ambiguity and equivocation.

The defective argument is as follows.

(1) If we think of something, we must conceive of it.
(2) What we conceive of is a conception.
(3) A conception is a mental entity in our own minds.
(4) Therefore, when we think of something, it is a mental entity in our own minds.

The mental entity may be described as an *idea* or, in more modern terms, as a *representation*. By the same argument, one might then

---

[2] J. Barwise and J. Perry, *Situations and Attitudes* (MIT Press, 1983), p. 241.

conclude that what a person thinks of is always some idea or representation. The plausibility of the argument, whether formulated in terms of conceptions, ideas, or representations, is the same, but it is worth having all the arguments before us.

In terms of ideas the argument is as follows.

(1I) If we think of something, we must have an idea of it.
(2I) What we have an idea of is an idea.
(3I) An idea is a mental entity in our own mind.
(4I) Therefore, when we think of something, it is a mental entity in our our mind.

In terms of representations, the argument is as follows.

(1R) If we think of something, we must represent it.
(2R) What we represent is a representation.
(3R) A representation is a mental entity in our own mind.
(4R) Therefore, when we think of something, it is a mental entity in our own minds.

The equivocation occurs in the second and third premisses. Suppose that I think of a cat, my own cat Sandy. If I think of Sandy or have any belief about Sandy, then, as the first premiss affirms, I must conceive of, have an idea of, or represent Sandy. But notice that what I thus conceive of is a particular furry feline, a living material body. When we turn to the second premiss of each argument, the premiss may appear obviously true or obviously false depending on which meaning of the last word in the sentence we understand. If, for example, by *conception, idea, or representation* we mean the mental operation, then the premiss is obviously false in the case in question. What I conceive of, have an idea of, or represent, when I think of Sandy, is not a mental operation but a furry feline. He is no mental operation, in this sense, no conception, idea, or representation. So to make the second premiss true, *conception, idea*, and *representation* must be used in a special philosophical sense of these words to refer to the object of the mental operation.

Of course, the problem then arises concerning the third premiss. For this premiss is only plausible if the term in question is used to refer to a mental operation. That sense would, however, render the second premiss false, as we have noted. So we must use the other sense of the terms, in which they refer to the object of the mental operation. But then there is no reason to assume the truth of the third premiss. There is no reason to suppose that Sandy is a mental entity in my mind. Thus, the plausibility of the argument depends on interpreting *conception, idea*, and *representation* as referring to a mental operation in the second premiss and as referring to the object of that operation in the third premiss, in order to render those premisses true. The argument rests on the fallacy of equivocation.

Argument against intermediaries

To clear the way for his theory of conception and belief, Reid offered an argument against the theory that we conceive of objects by conceiving of ideas, representations, or the like. We have already considered Reid's criticism of the argument to show that what we conceive of is always some idea, conception, or representation, but to refute an argument for a view is not the same as to refute the view. Reid did, however, have an argument against the theory of intermediaries which has some contemporary import.

The theory of intermediaries attempts to explain how we conceive of an object in terms of our conceiving of an idea or representation that signifies the object. If, however, we conceive of an object by conceiving of an idea or representation signifying the object, then we must be able to interpret the sign, that is, understand what the sign signifies. For, if we do not understand what the sign signifies, we cannot conceive of the object signified by conceiving of the sign. Therefore, we cannot explain how we conceive of an object in terms of our conceiving of an idea or representation, since in order to explain how we understand the sign we must already assume that we conceive of the object.

Reid notes, moreover, that when he attentively reflects, he can find no idea or representation when he conceives of an object. Thus, the empirical evidence of introspective reflection is contrary to the theory of intermediaries. Given that we can conceive of things that are not ideas or representations, evidence that we conceive of these things by conceiving of ideas or representations must be empirical, and the empirical evidence of reflection is to the contrary. It is clear that Reid thought that there was no other empirical evidence that supported the theory either. If we cannot explain how we conceive of objects by postulating ideas or representations, and if there is no direct empirical evidence of the existence of those ideas or representations, then, by the principle of parsimony, we should not assume that they exist. Thus, the arguments that Reid offers against the theory of representational intermediaries are, in effect, that such intermediaries are otiose from the standpoint of explanation and that there is no empirical evidence for their existence. Consequently, the postulation of their existence is unwarranted.

Conception, belief, and intentionality

Let us now turn to Reid's positive theory of belief. For Reid, the objects of a conception or belief are precisely those things which I have some conception of or belief in. If I conceive of my cat Sandy, it is Sandy and not some idea or representation of Sandy that is the object of my conception. If, moreover, I believe that Sandy is a cat, I conceive that Sandy is a cat, a proposition, and I affirm what I thus conceive. To conceive that Sandy is a cat, I conceive of Sandy, I conceive of the attribute of being a cat, and I conceive of the former having the latter.

This theory might appear to lead to some difficulty when I believe something of a thing that does not exist, for example, when I believe that Pegasus is a horse. Reid thought that this was not a problem at all. Reid noted the intentionality of thought, though he did not call it that. He considered it to be one of the postulates of human psychology that people conceive of things that do not exist at that moment, when they remember them for example, and, moreover, that they conceive of things that never existed. Furthermore, just as we conceive of things that do exist immediately, without the intermediary of ideas or representations, so we conceive of things that do not now exist, or things that never existed, immediately, without the intermediary of ideas or representations. Thus, according to Reid, I may immediately conceive of Pegasus and affirm of Pegasus the property of being a horse.

Reid regarded it as obvious that we could conceive of things that did not exist. He actually went further than this, beyond the doctrine of Brentano, who read Reid, to that of Meinong, as Routley has noted.[3] Reid clearly thought that there could be truths

---

[3] See a recently discovered essay, F. Brentano, 'Was an Reid zu loben: Ueber die Philosophie von Thomas Reid', *Grazer Philosophische Studien*, 1 (1975), 1–18; and also D. Schultess, *Philosophie et sens commun chez Thomas Reid* (Berne, 1983); R. Routley, *Exploring Meinong's Jungle and Beyond: An Investigation of Noneism and the Theory of Items* (Canberra, 1980), *passim*.

about things that did not exist, most obviously the truth of the non-existence of such things. Moreover, he thought that the solution to the traditional problem of universals was that universals did not exist but that we could conceive of them and affirm them of particulars. Reid was a particularist in his ontology. He thought that everything that existed was either a particular individual or a particular quality of an individual. Universals, which are not particulars, do not exist. Yet, our beliefs involve the affirmation of universals that do not exist of individuals, sometimes of individuals that exist and sometimes of individuals that do not exist. The affirmation of the property of being a horse of Pegasus is the affirmation of a universal that does not exist of an individual that does not exist, but the belief that Pegasus is a horse is, nevertheless, true, while the beliefs that Pegasus is a dog or that Pegasus exists are false.

2. A MODERN REFORMULATION

Belief and opacity

It will be useful to formulate Reid's theory of belief in a more precise manner than Reid actually did in order to examine the consequences more fully. Noting that, for Reid, an object of conception may be something that does not exist, the theory would be as follows. S believes that o is F if and only if some object of conception x and some attribute of being A are such that S conceives of x as o, S conceives of being A as being F, and S attributes being A conceived as being F to x conceived as o. This analysis has a Fregean flavour, for to conceive of something as something is a way, or mode, of conceiving it, though, for Reid, the objects thus conceived may, like Pegasus, not exist. Thus, we might give a paraphrase of the above analysis by saying that S believes that o is F if and only if some object of conception x and some attribute of being A are such that S conceives of x under the mode of conception o^*, S conceives of being A under the mode of conception F^* and S attributes being A under the mode of conception F^* to x under the mode of conception o^*. The terms that replace o and F refer to an object of conception and an attribute respectively, but they also refer to a mode of conceiving the object and a mode of conceiving the attribute respectively.[4]

[4] B. Loar, 'Reference and Propositional Attitudes', *Philosophical Review*, 84 (1972), 43–62.

The theory, even at this elementary level of exposition, is adequate to explain the opacity of belief sentences under a *de dicto* reading. Consider the following sentences so construed.

(1) Alexander believes that Sandy is a pussy-cat.
(2) Alexander believes that Lehrer's only pet is a pussy-cat.
(3) Alexander believes that Lehrer's only pet is a *Felis domesticus*

Suppose that (1) is true and both (2) and (3) are false, though Sandy is Lehrer's only pet and the attribute of being a pussy-cat is the attribute of being a *Felis domesticus*. The reason is that Alexander has met Sandy on the street and read his name-tag, but Alexander does not have any idea how many pets Lehrer has or that there is an attribute of being a *Felis domesticus*. Some object of conception *x* and some attribute of being *A* are, therefore, such that Alexander conceives of *x* as Sandy, Alexander conceives of being *A* as being a pussy-cat, and Alexander attributes being *A* conceived as being a pussycat to *x* conceived as Sandy. On the other hand, Alexander does not conceive of any object of conception as Lehrer's only pet or any attribute as being a *Felis domesticus*. The explanation of opacity is that there are different ways of conceiving an object and an attribute. Whether a *de dicto* belief sentence is true, on Reid's theory, depends on how one conceives of *o* and *F* on the mode of conception of an object and attribute, as well as on the object and attribute conceived. To conceive of something in terms of the meaning of some words is to conceive of it in a certain way. This is not to say that to conceive of something is to conceive of some words that signify it, though we may conceive of something in this way. It is only to claim that the meanings of words are ways of conceiving of things.

Meaning

Reid says that to conceive of an attribute or universal is to conceive of the meaning of a general term. This is not to say that to conceive of an attribute of something is to conceive of some word that signifies the attribute, though we may conceive of an attribute in this way. Meanings of words are ways of conceiving. This doctrine has the consequence that a person may conceive of something in a certain way, in terms of the meaning of some predicate, when he does not know exactly what the meaning is, and, consequently, does not know exactly how he conceives of it. Putnam has made similar observations.[5] Since Putnam has indicated that he is a student of Reid, it is a question of some interest as to whether his theory was inspired by his study of Reid.[6] Be that as it may, Reid held that many of our conceptions, those constituting the meaning of general terms, were what he called conceptions of conceptions. We learn the meaning of these terms, Reid averred, by a kind of induction concerning what others mean, and we mean by those terms what those who are most expert in the language mean by them. These conceptions, he says, are like pictures of pictures. This is, of course, the division-of-labour theory of meaning.

One objection to this theory is that, given Reid's theory of belief, it implies that people do not know exactly what they believe. It seems, on the contrary, that people do, in fact, know what they believe, even though they do not know exactly what others mean by the words they would use to express their beliefs. A second objection is that a person may believe that he sees an object having a perceptual quality, and, indeed, know that he believes this, without knowing the meaning others assign to any general word describing the quality. Reid had an answer to these objections. His answer to the first objection is contained in his answer to the second. Reid distinguished between general conceptions of attributes common to a number of objects and conceptions of particular qualities, qualities of one object only. The general conceptions we learn from others. They are conceptions of common attributes or universals. Conceptions of some particular qualities we learn as the result of our natural constitution by means of innate principles of the mind.

Armed with this distinction, we may reply to the second objection formulated above. A person may believe that an object he sees has a particular quality without knowing the meaning others assign to any general word describing the quality. His belief concerns a particular quality of that object only and not an attribute that is common to other objects. Since language serves the purposes of communica-

---

[5] H. Putnam, 'Meaning and Reference', *Journal of Philosophy*, 70 (1983), 699–711. The question naturally arises as to whether Reid, like Putnam, held that the meaning of natural-kind terms involved some relation to external objects and qualities and thus was not entirely in the mind. It is clear that Reid thought that meaning arose from such relations, but it is less clear whether he thought that such relations were in any way constitutive of the meaning.

[6] H. Putnam, foreword to N. Daniels, *The Geometry of Visibles and the Case for Realism* (New York, 1974).

tion, the predicates and adjectives of the language concern common attributes, and the language lacks names for qualities that are the qualities of one object only. This does not mean that we could not have a predicate naming such a quality. Such predicates would simply lack utility. They would be useless for purposes of communication.

What of the meaning of those predicates signifying common attributes or universals? Would Reid accept the consequence that we conceive of something we know not what? Reid thought it important to distinguish between those conceptions that are clear and distinct and those that are only relative and obscure. We may have a clear and distinct conception, when we have some exact definition of the attribute conceived, in geometry for example. But we may, and often do, have a relative conception only, as being some quality, we know not what, referred to by others by some word in the language. Between these two extremes we may have some more or less exact conception. The consequence of this theory of conception for a theory of belief is that if meanings and conceptions may be more or less clear and distinct, more or less relative and indistinct, the same is true of the beliefs.

Truth conditions

It would, of course, be anachronistic to ask how Reid understood the truth conditions for belief sentences on the basis of this theory, for he did not raise or discuss that question directly. His theory, however, implies a distinction between what is in the mind of the believer and what determines the truth of a belief sentence. Consider the sentence, 'Lehrer believes that Aker committed a criminal offence'. I am no expert in the law, and I do not have any clear idea of what constitutes a criminal offence in the eyes of the law. My conception of what it means is that it refers to an offence against the law for which a person could be punished by imprisonment. This is a very inadequate conception of a criminal offence. It is not, of course, the sort of conception that a lawyer or judge would have.

Now if I say, 'Aker committed a criminal offence', since I mean by 'criminal offence' what the experts, that is, lawyers and judges mean, the truth conditions for the sentence depend on what the experts mean. What is in my mind is only the inadequate conception of what the experts mean. Moreover, I know that my conception is inadequate and, knowing this, I know that I do not know exactly what the truth conditions for the sentence are, except that they are something, I know not exactly what, determined by what the experts mean by 'criminal offence'. Consider again the belief sentence, 'Lehrer believes that Aker committed a criminal offence'. What I affirm is that Aker has the attribute of having committed a criminal offence, and my conception of a criminal offence is relative to that of others. My belief would be true if and only if Aker had the attribute meant by lawyers and judges by the term 'criminal offence', for I mean what they mean. To specify the truth conditions for the sentence one would need to know something more than what is in my mind. One would need to know something about what is in the minds of lawyers and judges. The meaning of 'criminal offence' that determines the truth value of the sentence is not in my mind, but there is a meaning that is in my mind that refers to a meaning in the minds of others, and *that*, supplemented with causal relations perhaps, determines the truth conditions.

Consciousness

We now turn to a central doctrine of Reid's philosophy of mind, that of the faculty of consciousness. By a faculty, Reid meant an innate power of the mind to perform certain operations. He held that there was a faculty of consciousness by means of which we automatically conceived of the operations of our own minds, for example, conceiving and believing. How can we know what we conceive by consciousness if we conceive something we know not what? The answer depends on the distinction between an act of thought, whether conceiving or believing, and the object of the act. What we know from consciousness is the character of the act of the thought, the way we think of the object. The way in which we conceive of an object is a mode of conception, a modification or feature of the conceiving. All of this we know from consciousness.

When I know from consciousness what I conceive or believe, this is not because the object of conception or belief is the object of consciousness; in many cases the object of conception is something external to the mind. It is because the operations of conceiving and believing as well as the modes and features of those operations are objects of consciousness. The modes of conceiving and believing determine directly, or indirectly by reference to the conceptions of others, the objects of these operations. It is clear that Reid anticipated an adverbial theory of conception. To conceive of an object is to conceive in a certain way. He is, in this respect, rather close to Sellars, who, like Reid, affirms that to conceive of a universal is to conceive of the meaning of a general word.[7]

When I believe that Aker has committed a criminal offence, I have a conception of the legal conception of a criminal offence, and that suffices for the truth of my belief to be determined by the legal conception. It may be the case that my conception of that conception is somewhat inadequate, but it is my conception of that conception that I know from consciousness of my mental operations. My conception of that conception is not sufficient for clear and distinct knowledge of the truth conditions for my belief. I do, of course, know that my belief is true if and only if Aker committed a criminal offence. So, there is a sense in which I do know the truth conditions, but this is not clear and distinct knowledge. It is that kind of knowledge of the truth conditions of the belief that is compatible with my not knowing who Aker is or what a criminal offence is. Clear and distinct understanding and knowledge of the truth conditions presupposes that I know what a criminal offence is, that I could specify a precise definition of the word. A lawyer could, perhaps, do that, and his understanding of what I believe would have greater clarity and distinctness than my understanding of what I believe. Clarity and distinctness admit of degrees, of course, but the point remains that another person may have a clearer conception of what I believe than I do, though I must have some conception of what I believe. That is guaranteed by consciousness.

Consciousness and signification

It will be useful to say something more about Reid's conception of consciousness and signification. Reid contended that there were various faculties of the human mind that yielded conception and belief. The faculty of perception yields the conception of and belief in the existence of presently existing objects of sense, external material objects. The conception of and belief in the existence of the external objects is occasioned by sensations. Both the sensation and the conception are operations of the mind, but the sensations signify the objects conceived. They are mental signs. Moreover, they signify some of what they do as the result of innate principles of our natural constitution. Thus, sensations constitute an original

---

[7] W. F. Sellars, *Science, Perception and Reality* (London, 1963).

language which we understand without the instruction of man. A sensation of smell, for example, signifies a quality in the object that gives rise to the sensation, and it is an original sign.

I shall not here further elaborate Reid's theory of innate principles of the human mind. It is only essential to notice that Reid held that there must be some such principles, some original and natural signs, or we would be unable to learn the meaning of conventional and artificial signs that were the inventions of man. The relevance of these remarks for an understanding of consciousness is simply that consciousness is also a faculty of the mind, which, according to Reid, implies that it yields conception and belief in response to original or natural signs interpreted by innate principles. In the case of consciousness, the signs are the operations of the mind. Sensations, for example, in addition to signifying some external object, signify themselves. The sensation of smell, in addition to signifying a quality of an external object, signifies itself. Similarly, the mental operation of conceiving of an external object, whether clear and distinct or relative and obscure, signifies itself. Consciousness is the faculty that interprets these operations as signifying themselves. We could imagine creatures who had sensations but no conception of their sensations or other operations of their own minds. They would lack the faculty of consciousness.

Objections and replies

There are, of course, natural objections to this theory of consciousness. It leads to the conclusion that we are conscious of all the operations of our minds. It appears to lead to a regress. Let us consider first the claim that Reid's theory of consciousness leads to the conclusion that we are conscious of all the operations of our minds. It is natural enough to maintain, to the contrary, that at least some operations of the mind are not conscious. Reid claims that this is absurd. Operations of the mind are thoughts, and it is as absurd to suppose that there are unconscious thoughts as that there are unthought thoughts. Part of the explanation for Reid's doctrine is that he is a dualist. Reid would not have denied that there were states of the body, even of the brain, that were functionally related to thoughts, or operations, of the mind, but he would not have regarded those functionally related states as thoughts, or operations, of the mind.

Consciousness and the mental

I suggest the following justification for the claim that a state is mental only if we are conscious of it. There are many states of the body that are functionally related to thoughts and beliefs that are clearly not operations of the mind. At the present moment, for example, there are processes going on in my stomach, secretions of fluids, for example, which are functionally related to my having thoughts of food, just as there are processes going on in my eyes which are functionally related to thoughts of words before my eyes. These processes in my stomach and eyes are not operations of the mind. Moreover, Reid argued, the mere fact that some of those processes occur in the nerves or brain, rather than the eyes or stomach, provides no argument for regarding them as operations of the mind. Something is a thought, or mental operation, only if it is conscious, and if it is conscious, then consciousness gives us a conception and belief of the existence of it. In short, then, not every state of the body that is functionally related to thought is a thought, not even every state of the brain that is functionally related to thought is a thought, so why not accept consciousness as the demarcation line between thought, which is what Reid meant by a mental operation, and those physical processes that are only functionally related to thought?

There is an obvious reply to the foregoing rhetorical question, to wit, that the assumption of unconscious mental operations provides the best explanation of certain mental processes. In general, Reid rejects hypotheses that merely enable inference of the best explanation. Following Newton, he accepts the principle that such hypotheses are to be accepted only if there is independent evidence of the existence of the explaining cause and the cause has been shown to be adequate to explain the effect. In the case of unconscious thoughts, Reid would regard it is as obvious that the independent evidence of the existence of the explaining cause is missing.

There is, however, another line of reply by Reid. It is based on a distinction between consciousness and attentive reflection. Reid says that we are conscious of all the operations of our minds but that we attentively reflect on very few of them. Reid notes that there are many things which we see but do not notice or reflect upon at all. Similarly, we are conscious of many operations of our own minds which we do not notice or reflect upon at all; Reid's favourite examples are sensations that go unnoticed. In both cases, according to Reid, we have a conception and belief of the existence of the things in question, sensations for example, but those conceptions and beliefs, being of no interest to us, are immediately forgotten. The evidence that we have such conceptions and beliefs is that, if we learn to direct attention to them, we can study them and remember what they are like. Reid's assumption is clear. If the mind does not yield a conception and belief of the existence of those states, then no amount of directing our attention toward them will yield knowledge of those states. I can direct my attention toward my eyes or stomach, but that does not give me knowledge of the internal states of those organs when I have no conception of the states of those organs. Conception of mental states is, Reid contended, automatic, the product of consciousness, whether we attend to it or not. Mental states are automatically processed by consciousness as is other incoming information.

Regress of consciousness

Let us now turn to the problem of the regress. Reid is clearly sensitive to regress problems. He discusses the volition-regress problem in detail. He says nothing of a regress problem with respect to consciousness, however. He clearly did not discern that there was a problem. How might such a regress arise? Suppose I think of a colour. According to Reid, I then have a conception of this mental operation, the thinking, because consciousness automatically supplies me with a conception and belief of my mental operations. But the conception of the thinking is also a mental operation, and, therefore, I must have a conception of this conception. Consciousness automatically supplies me with a conception and belief of my mental operations. But this conception of a conception is also a mental operation. I must have a conception of it, and so on *ad infinitum*.

Why did Reid not mention this regress? I think that the answer is simply that he thought that consciousness supplied us with a conception of the *other* operations of the mind. Thus, if I perceive or remember or reason, consciousness provides me with a conception of those mental operations, but consciousness does not provide me with a conception of the mental operations of consciousness. That is not to say that we cannot learn to reflect upon the operations of consciousness and, as a result, know that we are conscious and that consciousness provides us with a conception of our other mental operations. But this knowledge concerning consciousness is not automatic. It is the result of reflecting attentively upon it, something that we do not ordinarily do. This reply would not be *ad hoc*. It has an empirical basis. As a matter of fact, everyone automatically knows that they feel or think when they do, but not everyone knows that they are conscious of thought and feeling when they are. They know the latter only when their attention is directed to the fact.

Consciousness and intentionality

I shall now articulate the most important aspect of Reid's theory of consciousness, the implied relationship between consciousness and intentionality. In so doing, I shall proceed beyond Reid's own exposition to examine the undeveloped consequences of his theory. The two aspects of the human mind that are the most salient and the most puzzling in contemporary philosophy of mind are intentionality and consciousness. These two features of the human mind are, on Reid's theory, closely related. Our understanding of signification is the result of consciousness. When we feel or think, we are conscious of these operations of the mind. Our consciousness of these operations yields a conception of our feeling or thought and a belief that they exist. Given the operations of consciousness, the feeling or thought signifies itself, for it automatically gives rise to a conception and belief of the existence of itself. Notice, however, that in this case of signification, the sign, the thing signified, and the operation of the mind by virtue of which the former signifies the latter to us are all objects of consciousness. They are transparent to consciousness. As a result, we obtain an understanding of this relation of signification. This relation is, of course, not restricted to a relation between mental operations, since signs, sensations, for example, also signify other things, external qualities and objects. Our understanding of signification, and, consequently, of intentionality, is a product of consciousness.

It is important not to confuse the foregoing claim with the quite different claim that signification and intentionality are the products of consciousness. It is our *understanding* of signification and intentionality that are the products of consciousness. Thus, we can imagine beings, the brutes, for example, that are not conscious, though they are endowed with feeling and thought. They will have thoughts and feelings, but they will have no conception of their thoughts and feelings. Consequently, they will not think about thoughts, though they may think about other things, frogs, for example. They will have mental operations, but they will have no conception of them. Consciousness is essentially a metafaculty. Such brutes may also understand signs, that is, they may conceive of what the signs signify. They will lack, however, any conception of the relation of signification. They will understand what a sign signifies, but they will not understand signification.

There is one important consequence of understanding the relation of signification. As a result, we can *assign* signification to a sign, and we can *alter* the signification of the sign. In short, our understanding of signification renders the operations of our minds semantically plastic. A being that responds to signs but does not understand signification cannot decide to let a sign signify something, for it does not understand what it is for a sign to signify anything. Such a being may respond to signs, may understand what they signify, but it will be semantically rigid. It cannot alter the signification of the signs it understands. To do this, it would need to understand signification, an understanding that is the product of consciousness.

Our peculiarity is not that we have minds with intentional states and operations. It is that we have the capacity to bestow and create intentionality, to bestow and create reference, because we understand signification. Consciousness is a necessary condition of that understanding, according to Reid. It is clear that Reid articulated a causal, or transmission, theory of signification. As a result of learning words from others, we mean what they mean, but the original assignment of meaning to words, as well as the decision to agree to what others mean, presupposes that we understand meaning as well as meanings. The transmission of meaning and reference is not automatic. We agree to mean what others mean, and to agree to this we must understand meaning. If we did not, we would not understand that the words of others have meaning, though, of course, we might understand what they mean.

Reid contended that we must understand certain signs without instruction as the result of our natural constitution, or it would be impossible for us to learn the meaning of artificial signs. He thought that we understood certain gestures, expressions of the face, and modulations of the voice as the result of innate principles. These are the language of nature, which we understand automatically and without tutelage. As a result, we understand what people intend, and, consequently, we can agree to mean what others mean by certain artificial signs. The basis of conventional language is the language of nature. We have some understanding of what others mean by nature, but an understanding of meaning is given to us by consciousness. Reid postulated those innate principles which he took to be necessary to our obtaining the understanding we have. He thought that nature would be frugal in her gifts, and, therefore, postulated the *minimum* he thought must be innate in order to account for our conceptions and beliefs. Most of our conceptions, all our general conceptions, are products of man, not of nature, as man parcels the objects of nature into classes to suit his needs. This results in the conception of universals which we use to sort the objects and qualities we perceive into kinds.

Belief and reason

I shall conclude my reformulation of Reid's theory by mentioning his distinction between reason and the other faculties. As we have noted, Reid thought that certain of our faculties, perception, for example, yielded conception and belief as an automatic response to sensory stimulation. These beliefs arise from innate principles of the human mind. These principles cannot be proven to be trustworthy without arguing in a circle, but, in fact, it is a first principle that such principles are not fallacious, and, therefore, no man can disbelieve his faculties. Reason may, of course, lead us to opposite conclusions, but reason is no match for nature, and we believe what our nature dictates. Though we cannot prove first principles, neither is proof necessary. The reason we cannot prove them is that proof assumes that reason is trustworthy, and we have no better reason for supposing reason to be trustworthy than any of our other faculties.

Arguments against perception, for example, are defective. Perception is not deceptive. To argue from the relativity of the observer, from the diversity of appearance, to the conclusion that we do not perceive material objects, for example, is fallacious. If we really do perceive the material object as perception convinces us we do, then an elementary knowledge of perspective, of the geometry of vision, teaches us that the object must present us with diverse appearances. This is no proof of the veracity of perception, for our beliefs about vision depend on the beliefs of perception. But once we admit the trustworthiness of our faculties, we find confirmation for the trustworthiness of perception in experience. If we do not admit the trustworthiness of our faculties, we are deprived of all knowledge and must be satisfied with total scepticism. Our nature keeps us from this alternative. It is the natural role of reason to certify the beliefs of nature and to extrapolate from them. It is not the role of reason to sit in judgement upon them and make war with them.

Here again, we find the importance of a metaprinciple, a principle about the first principles of our faculties, to wit, that they are trustworthy. But to have a conception of our faculties, of those trustworthy natural operations of the mind, we must have a conception of those operations. Once again, this is the gift of consciousness. It is consciousness that gives us knowledge of our mental operations, our conceptions and beliefs, and, therefore, enables us to extrapolate from those initial beliefs of our nature to the grandest artifices of science. Without consciousness, we might think and believe. We would, however, not know that we did, and, remaining ignorant of those initial beliefs, we would be prisoners of nature. It is consciousness that is the source of our inferential plasticity just as it is the source of our semantic plasticity. The special feature of the human mind is that it is a metamind. Without consciousness, we would lack this feature. We would be mentally rigid.

3. BEYOND DUALISM

Modern implications

Reid held that the contents of all of our beliefs that predicated some general attribute to a subject presupposed consciousness. It is consciousness that supplies us with a conception of our mental operations and, therefore, makes possible the creation of common attributes or universals, the meanings of general words. Such creation presupposes our conceiving of our mental operations and, indeed, those of others, and this conception is metamental. The moral for contemporary philosophy of mind is that our beliefs involving predication of some common attribute or universal to a subject depend on higher-level mental processes—in the terms of artificial intelligence, on central processing. Reid seems to me to have been entirely correct in this. Simple input models of belief are inadequate to give an account of the most simple beliefs with any general content, even when the generality is confined to the predicate. To notice the particular movement of some object, it may be sufficient to perceive that object. To believe that the object has an attribute of movement that is common to other objects requires a generalization from the particular conception of movement to a general conception of motion, from the particular to the universal. Thus, to generalize, one must have a general conception based on one's conception of particulars, and such a conception is metamental.

Reid did present us with a conception of input-system beliefs, perceptual beliefs occasioned by sensations confined in content to a particular quality of a particular object. Indeed, Reid articulated a theory of the faculties of the mind, faculties including the senses, memory, and language, that resembles contemporary modularity theory.[8] It is generality beyond the particular that requires higher-order operations of the mind. But that includes all the beliefs and knowledge we communicate to others in everyday life and scientific activity. Reid's theory is opposed to those theories of belief and knowledge based on the sort of information contained in a barometer, such as those of Dretske and Armstrong.[9] The objection is not that the barometer contains no information; it is that it is unable to understand that information. It is an uninterpreted sign. The interpretation of the sign, the understanding of information required to convert it into characteristic human knowledge and belief, presupposes the metamental operations of consciousness and generalization.

Reid would object to any contemporary theory of the mind defending a functional theory of semantic interpretation or intentionality of thought.[10] His argument, as indicated above, is that any operation on properties that are not intentional will not yield intentionality. To understand what a sign signifies we must be able to conceive of the object, whether that object presently exists, has existed, never existed, or even could not exist, or else we do not and

---

[8] See J. A. Fodor, *The Modularity of Mind* (MIT Press, 1983).

[9] F. Dretske, *Knowledge and the Flow of Information* (MIT Press, 1981); D. M. Armstrong, *Belief, Truth and Knowledge* (Cambridge UP, 1973).

[10] See J. R. Searle, *Intentionality: An Essay in Philosophy of Mind* (Cambridge UP, 1983).

could not understand the sign. Reid contended, on introspective grounds, moreover, that some such conceptions were immediate and the result of innate principles of the mind. These conceptions supply us with the means of interpreting certain original signs, without which we should be unable to learn the meaning of artificial signs in conventional languages.

The upshot, for Reid, is that conception, being intentional, is a primitive operation of the mind that is not reducible to any functional relationship. It is notable that Reid objected to the doctrine of the causal interaction between the mental and the physical on the grounds that it would lead to materialism, to functionalism, for example. It was his claim, in my opinion clearly confirmed by subsequent developments, that no functional relations could give an account of the intentionality of mind. No set of operations yields conception or intentionality unless one of those operations has intentional properties. One may, of course, argue that such properties are, in some sense, illusory, but Reid contended, again rightly in my opinion, that we know that our thoughts and conceptions are intentional. Consciousness gives us immediate knowledge of intentional operations of the mind. To deny intentionality for the sake of materialism is to argue for a theory against the facts. It is, moreover, unscientific to reject the facts of careful and controlled observation. Consciousness supplies us with knowledge of the existence of our thoughts and to some extent of the content of our thoughts.

Must we accept dualism and reject the computational theory of mind if we agree with Reid? On historical grounds, the answer would be affirmative. There is, however, a theory that avoids dualism and that is compatible with a great deal of what Reid has affirmed. This theory would admit an operation of the mind that had primitive intentional properties, but it would ascribe those properties to matter. We might call this *soft* materialism.[11] It incorporates two principles of intellectual modesty, to wit, that we should not prejudge what the properties of matter may be and that we should not deny the existence of properties we observe for the sake of scientific simplicity. To do so would be an abuse of the methodological principle of simplicity. It is, of course, possible that what we think we observe really does not exist. We are not, however, warranted in rejecting the intentional properties of mind

[11] See Searle, ibid.

as illusory simply because we cannot account for those properties in terms of a highly speculate theory of the human mind. We must have some independent reason for doubting the existence of those properties, and we do not have any such reason.

The final question is whether this means that we must deny a computational theory of the mind. If we so conceive of a computational theory that it disallows a primitive semantic or intentional property, that it allows only syntactical operations on syntactical properties, as Stich for example,[12] then, of course, Reid's theory, as well as soft materialism, is incompatible with a computational theory of the mind. Suppose, however, that we extend our conception of computational theory to admit such operations. Let us call this the *extended* computational theory of the mind. The soft materialist may hold that computational processes in the brain occurring below the level of consciousness occasion conception in the conscious mind. Reid himself contended that physical processes in the organs of sense and in the brain occasioned our conceptions of visible figures in a manner that suggests computation.

There is no reason to suppose that research in computational theories of the operations of the mind, research in artificial intelligence, for example, would be undermined by this alteration. Indeed, it might well be advanced. It would involve the admission that inorganic machines that imitate the working of the human mind may lack a property that the human mind possesses, one in terms of which the machine language is interpreted for human beings; but the programme of research would be otherwise unaffected. Rather than undermining the research programme, extended computational theory might free such research from the burden of trying to find some syntatic or functional property that *constituted* the semantic and international properties of humans.

Maybe we can produce a machine that imitates us perfectly, both internally and externally, without understanding the syntactic strings that it manipulates. Maybe we cannot. It depends on whether or not the semantic or intentional properties play some role in human inference and behaviour that cannot be successfully imitated by any other property. Whatever the outcome, the research programme based on current computational theory might be experimentally and computationally indistinguishable from that

[12] S. P. Stich, 'On the Ascription of Content', in A. Woodfield (ed.), *Thought and Object* (Oxford UP, 1982), pp. 153–206.

based on extended computational theory. Perhaps we shall find a model of consciousness in higher-order central processing. Perhaps we shall find that the organic character of the mind results in the emergence of properties not contained in inorganic machines of whatever complexity. Perhaps we shall find an explanation of consciousness in the central system of an organic machine. We are presently ignorant. We had better keep our metaminds open.[13]

[13] The research for this paper was supported by a grant from the National Science Foundation and a fellowship from the John Simon Guggenheim Memorial Foundation. I am indebted to Myles Brand, Stephen Shiffer and John C. Smith for critical comments on an earlier draft. I am also indebted to John C. Smith for research resulting in our co-authored paper, 'Reid on Testimony and Perception', in the *Canadian Journal of Philosophy*, Supplementary Issue (1985), to which the reader is referred for further clarification of Reid's views.

CHAPTER 4

TACIT BELIEF*

WILLIAM G. LYCAN

At this moment (even as I write), my wife Mary believes that my tie looks like a prize from the county fair coconut shy. This harsh observation occurred to her a few seconds ago, and she has just voiced it. ('That tie looks like a prize from the county fair coconut shy,' she said.) I have remonstrated, but she remains unshakeable in her conviction. She holds her belief candidly, militantly, and in so many words.

My wife also believes a number of other things, or so we might routinely suppose: that she is less than eighteen feet tall, that 10,329 > 10,328, and that snow in Stockholm does not instantaneously turn bright orange when it hits the ground. In fact, it seems she believes an *uncountable* number of other things—for example, that she is less than $6 + n$ ft. tall, for any positive real number n. But all these other beliefs differ crucially from her regrettable belief about my tie (and not just in truth value), for they have never occurred to her; she has never said any such thing to herself, and she is unaware that she has these beliefs, unless in a very rarefied sense of 'aware'. It is tempting to distinguish at least two kinds of belief: 'explicit' versus implicit or 'tacit'. Or perhaps conscious versus unconscious, occurrent versus dispositional, or the like. Some philosophers are content to let it go at that. Others add the suggestion that 'tacit' belief may be defined in terms of explicit belief or judgement, typically, as the *disposition* to judge,[1] but that is about as far as discussion goes.

My purpose in this paper is to argue that the distinction aimed at here is a vexed one at best, even granting that there is just one such distinction, and that serious work needs to be done if we are to carve doxastic reality at whatever joint(s) it may actually have. I shall

---

* © William G. Lycan 1986.
[1] e.g., Sellars (1958), p. 521, (1969); de Sousa (1971); more recently, Powers (1978), and Richardson (1981).

begin by sketching what I now consider a crude and neologistic notion of explicit belief, based on Lycan (1981) (cf. also Lycan (1985*a*)) and arguing for its replacement by a more accurate notion of 'occurrent' belief. Then I shall ask exactly what contrasting notion we really have of 'merely tacit' belief, and whether anything, in fact, answers to this label.

I. EXPLICIT BELIEF

I assume (having argued elsewhere) that William of Occam and Wilfrid Sellars are right in maintaining that we all talk silently to ourselves (Sellars (1956, 1967, 1969)). From time to time we make mental judgements, and judgings in this sense are inner episodes that have certain functions in our behavioural economies. What makes the judgement that *P* a *judgement* that *P* is its characteristic type of functional role; what makes it a judgement *that P* is its having a certain internal structure, its consisting of proper parts arranged in a certain way, and, in virtue of this, its bearing certain inferential relations to other possible or actual judgements and certain causal and/or teleological relations to things in the world. Crudely, to judge is to host and manipulate a representation, an inner formula of some sort that has both a distinctive causal surface and a semantic content.[2]

This sort of thing is going on in Mary. She represents my tie to herself, or at least she harbours what is in fact a representation of my tie, and this representation connects in a causally potent way with her concept of prizehood, a representation of the county fair (or perhaps just of the coconut shy itself), etc., the result being her tactless, overt speech act aforementioned; there may be further, non-verbal results as well, if I am not careful to make my own visits to the dry-cleaner. A specific state of her is correlated in a referential way with my tie, another state of her with prizehood, another with the fair, and so on, and these in turn are correlated with some other concepts having ominous normative and even visceral features.

However the details may go, it is *not* this sort of thing that is going on in Mary with regard to the concept of being less than eighteen feet tall, or to the number 10,329 or the city of Stockholm. There is

---

[2] The crucial distinction between these two features of the representation, and the importance of respecting both, is stressed in Lycan (1981, 1985*a*).

no plausible sense in which these things are represented explicitly within her at this very moment, much less linked up with the other relevant concepts in even a quiescent way. (For one thing, since the human brain is a finite device, it is unlikely to be able to represent each of non-denumerably many propositions.) In particular, she never episodically *judges* that she is less than eighteen feet tall or the like. So in Lycan (1981) I identified 'explicit' belief with judging and 'tacit' belief with the disposition to judge.

However, to frame the difference in that way is to make it a distinction between a kind of episode or *event* and a dispositional *state*, and now I think that is wrong or at least pointlessly neologistic. For, as several philosophers have pointed out (see, particularly, Hunter (1980) and Vendler (1972)), 'believe' is not an action-verb or an event-verb but a state-verb. Beliefs are not happenings; there are no datable events of 'believing that *P*', though there are datable events of judging or of *coming* to believe. So although our distinction between judging and being disposed to judge is itself perfectly sound, it seems that only the latter is properly called belief.

2. BELIEF STATES

Yet it is still natural to distinguish between explicit and tacit beliefs, even within the class of dispositional-belief states. At least, it is plausible to think that some belief states involve explicit representation in a way that other belief states do not; explicit representation may constitute part of the relevant dispositions' categorical bases. A paradigm case of this would be one in which a previously tokened representation is now stored quiescently in long-term memory. (Actually this is misleading usage. The original token was an event which is now past; *it* is not 'stored' anywhere. Rather, as one of its causal consequences, some sort of characteristic trace or formula having its same computational shape is stored.) The stored formula is accessible to various executive agencies and can be hauled out on cue, resulting in a new judgement or tokening bearing the same computational shape.

Notice that this state of affairs is an *occurrent* one despite its also having dispositional features. The subject actually and occurrently stores the representation over such-and-such a period of time. Even though no judging need be taking place and this actual storage is not an episode, it hardly merits the deprecatory label 'tacit'. Given that we have abandoned the older use of the term 'occurrent belief' as meaning *judgement*,[3] it seems entirely proper to reintroduce it as applying to such cases. In this sense, for example, people have occurrent beliefs even when they are asleep and hosting no mental events: sleeping people still have representations stored in long-term memory.[4]

Of course, there are still cases of (what people ordinarily call) believing that do not fit this new model of occurrent belief either. Indeed, my wife's beliefs about Stockholm *et al.* do not fit it, because the relevant representations never have previously been tokened and surely do not inhabit her long-term memory or any other department of her internal bureaucracy. So we must still try to posit a contrasting notion of 'tacit' belief. No great departure from our first attempt is required, however; we may still identify tacitly believing that *P* with being disposed to judge that *P* and to store the appropriate formula as a result.

Notice carefully that neither our original distinction between judging and being disposed to judge nor our new distinction between actual storage and being disposed to judge and store coincides with the difference between conscious and unconscious belief (cf. Armstrong (1973), pp. 7–8, and de Sousa (1971), p. 76). A person need not be conscious in order to have an occurrent belief in our new sense of actual storage; for that matter, a person need not be conscious of every judgement he or she makes. The occurrent/tacit distinction applies within the class of unconscious beliefs.[5]

---

[3] This older usage can be found in Sellars (1969), p. 514, de Sousa (1971), and Foley (1978), p. 312. A variant terminology is Harman's (1978), who uses 'occurrent' to mean *conscious*; this seems to me misleading (see the concluding paragraph of this section).

[4] Thus, beliefs can be occurrent without being occurren*ces*. It should be noted, though, that the existence of occurrent beliefs in our new sense is an empirical matter (and not just because the existence of sentient beings at all is an empirical matter); the representation-storage theory of cognition might turn out to be false, or, as Dennett (1981*b*) points out, the representations that human beings actually store might not correspond in any way to the beliefs attributed to subjects by common sense.

[5] Unless there is such a thing as a *conscious but tacit* belief, which I doubt. It is an interesting question whether we ever introspect beliefs. On both phenomenological and theoretical grounds I doubt that too; what we introspect, in the way of cognitive items, are judgements, and we infer our knowledge of our beliefs from those. (But cf. Vickers (1969)). NB, I do not mean to deny that there are unconscious mental occurrences.

Note that if there are tacit beliefs, then there are presumably also tacit desires,

3. THE PROBLEM

I wish we could leave the matter at that, but in fact we cannot, for there are counter-examples to the sufficiency of our new analysis of tacit belief, showing it to be too liberal. Here are two:

(1) *The opinionated man.* He is a Peircean, in that he abhors being agnostic on any subject, but not enough of a Peircean, in that in him the 'irritation of doubt' triggers not inquiry but a snap judgement. At least, on many occasions when he entertains a proposition for the first time, he immediately affirms the proposition or denies it, depending on what else is going on in his global psychology at the time. (Let us take 'global psychology' broadly here, to include any mental or neurophysiological condition that has psychological influence.) Thus, at a time t our subject has countless dispositions to judge—determined by his global psychology—but we would not count these as antecedently existing beliefs, however tacit.

(2) *The randomized-opinionated man.* He is like the first opinionated man, except that whether he affirms or denies the proposition he newly entertains at t is determined by an internal coin-flipper whose physical constitution and overall occurrent state at t grounds counterfactuals regarding what judgement the man would make at t concerning whatever proposition was next entertained.[6]

These examples show that not every disposition to judge, or even every position to judge and store, counts intuitively as a belief of any sort.[7] We need to find an additional necessary condition of

intentions, and other propositional attitudes. Lynne Rudder Baker has pointed out to me that a good theory of *tacit intentions* would help resolve the problem bruited in Kripke (1982) regarding the difference between computing *plus* and computing 'quus'.

[6] (2) is really a special case of (1), since the coin-flipper is part of the randomized-opinionated man's global psychology. These counter-examples work, more generally, against almost any simple dispositional account of belief, such as F. Ramsey's (1926) analysis in terms of dispositions to bet (our opinionated men may be betting men as well).

[7] Bas van Fraassen has asked me (in conversation) why we should not allow that the opinionated men *are* tacit believers in virtue of their readiness (after all) to judge, to bet, and so on. But the opinionated men themselves would disavow any standing tacit beliefs and acknowledge (perhaps with pride) that they had made up their minds

believing tacitly that P, presumably some restriction on the kind of categorical basis the relevant disposition to judge may have.[8]

4. EXTRAPOLATOR–DEDUCERS

An obvious move is to posit what Dennett (1975) calls an 'extrapolator–deducer', i.e. a device which operates on occurrently stored formulas, or 'core beliefs', and generates relatively obvious consequences of those occurrent beliefs when the occasions arises. Thus we might suggest that to believe tacitly that P is to be disposed to judge that P in virtue of the operation of one's extrapolator–deducer in drawing inferences from pre-existing core beliefs. This specification of the disposition's categorical basis rules out our opinionated men. It also has the virtue of revealing how appeal to tacit belief figures in the explanation of action. Public statements are the results of inner judgements, and judgements are (sometimes) the manifestations of dispositions to judge produced by the activity of the extrapolator–deducer that is the disposition's categorical basis. Public statements get made on newly bruited topics because their utterers have tacit beliefs, i.e., because the appropriate judgements are triggered by the utterers' extrapolator–deducers operating on core beliefs.

Two problems face this account, and both are serious.[9]

on the spot. ('Wasn't that a little bigoted of you?' 'Ah, get lost!') Further counter-examples are available: Foley (1978), p. 312 n, points out that, being a good introspector, I am disposed to assent to the proposition 'I am entertaining a proposition' whenever I entertain it, but surely I do not constantly tacitly believe it. Audi (1982) also suggests by implication that being disposed to judge is not necessary for tacit belief; intuitively, I believe every instance of '$n < 2$', where n is replaced by any member of the series, $1, 1\frac{1}{2}, 1\frac{3}{4}, 1\frac{7}{8} \ldots$, but since some of the later members of that series can be expressed in no less than millions of numerals, it is unlikely that I would assent to them if queried. (I suppose one might reply to this by insisting that due to the complexity of such expressions, I cannot really entertain them in the first place, and so they are no counter-example to the claim that if I were to entertain them, I would give my assent.)

[8] My problem here is not unrelated to that raised by Levi and Morgenbesser (1964). And cf. again Audi (1982). I am grateful to D. M. Armstrong, Stephen Stich and Alvin Goldman for the protracted discussion and criticism that for some reason were needed to make me see it at last.

[9] A third is raised by Dennett (1975): that the extrapolator–deducer will have to have tacit beliefs of its own and hence will require the services of a second extrapolator–deducer, which will in turn, etc. But I am not sure I see why the first extrapolator–deducer need have tacit beliefs. Dennett alludes to Lewis Carroll's problem of Achilles and the tortoise, but that problem in itself does not afflict any

First, we must find some way of restricting our analysans still further as regards the *range* of the extrapolator–deducer, for if we were to count just anything potentially deducible by the device as being tacitly believed, then we would have to suppose that every normal person tacitly believes all the provable theorems of arithmetic, all tautologies, and all the other consequences of his or her core beliefs. But surely the pre-theoretic concept of tacit belief does not stretch that far; not even tacit belief is closed under deduction. Intuitively, what we count as being tacitly believed at *t* are just those propositions which the extrapolator–deducer would infer *more or less immediately* if appropriately triggered at *t*.

The problem is to specify a type of 'immediacy' that sustains this intuition. Temporal immediacy suggests itself; we might try to count a proposition as tacitly believed provided the extrapolator–deducer were to spit it out within, say, one second of being queried. But this interpretation would introduce an unwanted parameter into our analysans. The *temporal* immediacy of an inference is relative to the intelligence or quick-wittedness of the subject who makes the inference; David Lewis's extrapolator–deducer spits out a good many more propositions in one second than mine does. Yet just in virtue of that difference in deducing-speed (let us drolly assume that Lewis and I are otherwise alike), we should not want to credit Lewis with holding tacit beliefs at *t* that I do not hold. What one believes, even tacitly, is not relative to one's intelligence.

A more natural and psychologistic interpretation of immediacy of inference would be a proof-theoretic one, couched in terms of the number of steps required for the derivation of a newly entertained proposition from core beliefs. A proposition would count as tacitly believed provided the extrapolator–deducer were to derive it in fewer than *n* steps. But the difficulty here is parallel and just as obvious. Length of derivation depends entirely (and pretty dramatically) on one's choice of a system of rules of inference; formula A may be S_1-derivable in two steps but S_2-derivable in no fewer than sixteen. Yet, as before, what one believes, even tacitly, is not relative to a choice of axiomatizations. Nor will it help to pursue the proof-theoretic strategy by specifying the logical systems *that the subject* (or the subject's brain) *actually uses*, for we do not, and perhaps cannot ever, know which system that is in fact; on the latter

extrapolator–deducer that is simply hard-wired to draw inferences of certain standard forms.

analysis we would never know what any subject tacitly believed.[10]

No further interpretation of immediacy occurs to me, so I shall give up for now and conclude this section by raising a closely related general point: immediacy, on any analysis, is going to be a matter of degree, like speed and length of derivation, and the degree of immediacy required by a given extrapolator–deducer theory of tacit belief will be chosen just in virtue of its correspondence to our intuitive ascriptions of tacit belief. That correspondence apart, however, the choice of such a cut-off point seems ontologically arbitrary. A subject whose judgement that P is produced with sufficient immediacy (in whatever sense) would count as antecedently having held the tacit belief that P, while a subject whose judgement that P is produced only slightly less immediately by an otherwise similar process would not, but would be described by the extrapolator–deducer theorist as having newly come to believe that P on the basis of having deduced it on the spot. But it seems wrong to suppose that what distinguishes a genuine (though tacit) believer at t from a non-believer at t is nothing but a slight variation in the value of a single unit of measurement, at least of any measurement of the sort likely to underlie the extrapolator–deducer theorist's, so long as we are supposing for the sake of discussion that tacit belief is a real, albeit dispositional, state of a subject and has causal powers.[11] Of course, we may later on want to question the latter assumption.

---

[10] Nor is ease of linear derivation all that is relevant to our judgements of tacit belief. Consider Powers's (1978) well-known trick question (slightly paraphrased here). 'Is there a four-letter English word ending in the letters *ee, enn, why*?' (The students search the alphabet for a few moments and reply 'No', or 'I don't think so'.) 'Is "deny" a four-letter English word ending in *ee, enn, why*?' 'Oh, yes.' It seems that the students tacitly believed that 'deny' was a four-letter etc., but did not even tacitly believe that *there was* a four-letter etc., even though the latter followed in one forehead-smackingly simple step of existential generalization from the former. (For brief discussion of Powers's example, see Castañeda (1980) and Boër and Lycan (1986).)

[11] Stephen Stich protests (in correspondence) that there are causal dispositions, such as brittleness, that are perfectly real, albeit matters of degree and vague at the edges. But where would vagueness of that sort be located, so to speak, in the ordinary concept of tacit belief? What seems to be a matter of degree on the extrapolator–deducer theory is the *tacitness*, not the fact of belief itself.

I suppose we could define a notion of believing-to-a-degree: It is true to degree d that S believes (tacitly) that $P =_{\text{def}} (\exists Q) (\exists! i) (S$ believes explicitly that Q & S's extrapolator–deducer would, if called to, deduce P from Q with immediacy i & i = degree d on the scale $(I_e, I_t))$, where I_e is the highest immediacy possible, I_t is the least immediacy allowed for a tacit-belief ascription to be even faintly plausible, and

5. FIELD'S PROPOSAL

An interesting variation on the extrapolator–deducer strategy is proposed by Field (1978), one that I think does eschew treating tacit belief as a real state of subjects. Though he cites Dennett (1975), Field does not himself explicitly invoke a deducing *device*; rather, he sees tacit beliefs as being simply the 'obvious consequences' of explicitly represented beliefs, letting this phrase stand on its own and evidently leaving ascribers of tacit belief to judge for themselves which consequences are 'obvious'. (Field notes that the vagueness of the notion of obviousness explains that vagueness of some of our intuitions about ascriptions of tacit belief.)

Now, again, it seems to me that if this proposal is right, then no tacit belief is a genuinely inner behaviour-causal state of a subject, and in particular a subject's tacit beliefs will be in the eye of the beholder, in that they will depend on what the beholder finds obvious. We would like to say that when Smedley first hears the question, 'Was Omaha vaporized by a 75-megaton hydrogen bomb in August of 1979?', and answers, 'No', this is *because* he has tacitly believed all along that no such tragedy occurred. If we are to continue in this vein, we cannot just observe that the answer 'No' is an obvious consequence of other things Smedley believes, for that alone would be no explanation, until supplemented by an account of Smedley's ability to *compute* obvious consequences of his explicit beliefs, which would bring us back to extrapolator–deducers again. On Field's proposal, for me to say of Smedley that he tacitly believes that no hydrogen bomb vaporized Omaha is for me to say no more than that Smedley has some explicit belief or other of which 'No hydrogen bomb vaporized Omaha' is *by my lights* an obvious consequence; I specify no inner state of Smedley. Further, the indexicality of the phrase 'by my lights' ensures that ascriptions of tacit belief will be true only relative to ascribers, since what is obvious to you may not be obvious to me. (Note that intelligence and quick-wittedness are not the only variables here. Even between

---

d is some value located appropriately towards the lower end of the scale. But (*a*) this is not the ordinary concept of tacit belief, or at least it is not easily expressible in ordinary language ('Does Steve believe that either there is a prime between 23 and 30 or he teaches philosophy in Iran?' 'Only to degree 0.05,'/'A little bit.') And (*b*) we still have all the problems of trying to specify the type of immediacy involved without introducing the unwanted relativities.

people of overall equal deductive ability, there are disparities in what they find obvious—vel-Introduction, for example.) We might strive for some more objective, non-person-relative notion of 'obviousness', but that would lead us back towards our proof-theoretic interpretation again. Or we might understand 'obvious' as meaning obvious *to the subject* rather than to the ascriber, but that would lead us back to the sad gap in the quick-wittedness between David Lewis and me.

For these reasons I do not not think Field's option will help us, though we should keep it in mind as a *deflationary* analysis of tacit belief should we come to desire one, more on which below.

6. EXTRAPOLATOR–DEDUCERS AND THE 'FRAME PROBLEM'

The second main difficulty facing the extrapolator–deducer strategy, which applies to Field's analysis as well, is this: if tacit beliefs are the counterfactual output of an extrapolator–deducer, what is the deducer's input? When Smedley instantly replies 'No' to our question about the nuclear obliteration of Omaha, we are to suppose this to be a result of the deducer's generating a judgement to that effect by inference from some set of explicitly represented premises—explicitly represented, that is, prior to Smedley's being asked. But it is hard to think of any specific premises that the average person *would carry around in his or her head* that entail Omaha's non-obliteration. 'Omaha exists today' or perhaps 'A relative of mine was living in Omaha in 1980' might serve, but these do not themselves entail that Omaha was not vaporized in 1979; we need the further premiss that *no one rebuilt* Omaha between August 1979 and January 1980, which, though reasonable, is surely not explicitly stored. 'No one has ever detonated a hydrogen bomb in the eastern half of the United States' is a possibility, I suppose, but I doubt that many people have ever explicitly represented that to themselves either. It is easy to come up with obvious truths which everyone (seemingly) believes and which entail that no hydrogen bomb vaporized Omaha, but (again) there is no evidence that ordinary people have ever represented any of them explicitly.[12]

---

[12] Several people have pointed out to me that the extrapolator might perform inductions as well as deductions. That would make the problem of the premises

I think it is this difficulty that makes some people sceptical about representationalism generally, or at least about the linear-deduction or theorem-proving model of information accessing which comes naturally to formal logicians but has been seen for at least a decade to be a non-starter *qua* realistic recipe for knowledge-representation by machines. In the light of what is sometimes called the 'frame problem',[13] one is tempted to reject the notion of explicit storage *tout court* and move towards a more thoroughly dispositional or holistic account of belief. But (*a*) I think there are fairly compelling reasons why we cannot reject core beliefs entirely (Lycan (1981), p. 154), and (*b*) *what* more 'thoroughly dispositional' account? If we are not behaviourists, our complete analysis of belief must specify some fairly characteristic aetiology for behaviour that is distinctive of belief, or face the usual counter-examples and charges of circularity and Turing-Test-ism (cf. Block (1981)).

What the extrapolator–deducer strategy has run smack into, I think, *is* the frame problem, in effect. To solve it, one must delimit some initial body of pre-set context-free background information and some ingenious mode of organization to be imposed on it, and then construct both a set of procedures for revising the background information under various conditions and a set of search and accessing processes, in such a way as to maximize one's machine's facility and accuracy in performing relatively novel tasks (or, more properly, to strike the optimal balance of facility against accuracy). Researchers in artificial intelligence (notably Minsky (1975), and Schank and Abelson (1977)) have abandoned the model involving a list of stored premisses plus a set of deductive-inference rules in favour of various non-linear modes of storage and styles of search involving 'frames', 'plans', templates, schemata, or the like, and various heuristics that operate on them; so, too, may we want, for psychological purposes, to replace our linear extrapolator–deducer

---

easier in principle, but I am still hard put to think of premisses even for an induction regarding New York *that are stored explicitly*. It is easy to reconstruct Smedley's reasoning in any of several ways, but all the ways that occur to me appeal to unrepresented premisses.

[13] See, e.g., Moore and Newell (1974), Minsky (1975), Winograd (1975, 1976), Winograd and Bobrow (1977), Lehnert (1979), Pylyshyn (1979), Dreyfus (1979), Fahlman (1979), and Dennett (1983). NB, I am not suggesting that the 'frame problem' is specific to tacit belief; it would arise even for a suitably large mass of explicitly stored belief.

with some other kind of extrapolator. If not frames, in Minsky's sense, perhaps we store stereotypes or even fuzzy global images of some sort. Smedley may extrapolate his newly explicit belief about Omaha, not by deducing it by steps from any set of premises, but by reading it off an image of an undisturbed middle America, green with lawn and white with picket fence, populated by pleasant, ordinary-looking (or more likely faceless) people going contentedly about their daily business. (There is plenty of psychological evidence for the claim that we think in stereotypes of some sort, typically, inaccurate ones; see, for example, Rosch (1977) and Nisbett and Ross (1980)). Thus, we *might* be able to save the extrapolator idea without running into our second difficulty, at least. On the other hand (cf. Lycan (1981), p. 157), some argument would have to be provided to show that Smedley's Reaganesque image did not itself constitute or contain a sentential representation—say, of the kind 'that middle America is undisturbed'—or something of that nature. There is such a thing as ideogrammatic writing, after all; some iconic representations are verbal as well.

Pending a breathtaking solution to the frame problem, however, I am pessimistic about the extrapolator strategy for the analysis of tacit belief. Alternative realistic accounts do not leap vibrantly to mind. But let us have one more try.

7. HAVING REASONS

In effect, our task is to explain why our opinionated men do not have tacit beliefs prior to making those snap judgements, given that all along they were *disposed* to make those judgements. What, intuitively, is wrong with the opinionated men? One salient feature that they share is that they are not rational—snap judgements are not considered or reasonable judgements, and, as seekers of reliable informants, you and I would set no store by the opinionated men's opinions. Perhaps this is why we do not perceive their judgements as manifesting antecedently held tacit beliefs.

We must be careful here. That a judgement is irrational, or unreasonable, does not (alas) entail that is not a genuine manifestation of belief. People say stupid things usually because they believe stupid things. So it is not the irrationality in the normative sense of the opinionated men's judgements that shows the men not to be true tacit believers. It is more that their judgements are not based on reasons at all, either good reasons or bad reasons. Evidence plays no role in their formation. So perhaps we can define belief as *the disposition to judge on the basis of reasons* (*good or bad*).

This would require an analysis in turn of the notion of 'basing'. Such analysis has been provided most notably in Swain (1981*a*, 1981*b*) and in Tolliver (1980) (see also Harman (1970), Armstrong (1973), ch. 6, Lehrer (1974), and Pappas (1981)). I cannot review the details here, but it is generally agreed that the notion of basing is a counterfactual or causal one: a belief *B* is based on a reasons *R* iff the subject would not have held *B* but for having *R*, or iff *R* figures appropriately in the causal ancestry of the subject's holding B, or some complex elaboration of one or both of these.

Notice that in order to understand such definitions we must have an antecedent understanding of what sorts of things 'reasons' are; otherwise the analysans may be far too easily satisfied. Paradigmatically, reasons are other beliefs and the causal ancestry in question is a process of inference, but Swain (1981*b*, ch. 3) argues compellingly for a broader notion of 'reason-states' that includes perceptual states, memory states, inner states such as pain that start off introspections, etc. We must simply agree on a list of such things— the *kinds* of things that can be reasons—before we ask and answer the question of what the basing relation consists in. So let us fall in with Swain's idea and accept his sort of list.

Having done so, let us now apply this notion of basing to our newly proposed definition of belief. If we take *inference from a prior belief* as our paradigm of what it is for something to be based on a reason, we immediately run into trouble: if to believe is to be disposed to judge on the basis of reasons, and if the paradigm of 'judging on the basis of reasons' is inferring from prior belief, then our account collapses back into the extrapolator theory and is subject to the same objections (the immediacy-specifying problem, and the difficulty of finding premisses). And it seems to me that similar objections could be raised for the sorts of reason-states I have mentioned: if a subject, appropriately stimulated, makes a judgement that is based on a perceptual state, on a memory state, or (through introspection) on a mental state of any other sort, how 'immediate' must the basing mechanism be if we are to count the resulting judgement as manifesting a prior tacit belief? And what, again, are the candidate reason-states for some of our recondite cases? Some plausible examples do come to mind, as in the case of my present belief that my office door is open behind me. I did just judge that my door was open due to my having recently and accessibly stored that perceptual information, and that makes it natural to say that since entering my office I have 'tacitly believed' the door to be open, even though there may have been no explicit representation to that effect actually stored anywhere with me (what is stored is just a perceptual memory trace, the *reason* for my subsequent judgement).

In addition, there are more counter-examples to the sufficiency of our present analysans:

(3) *The rationalizing opinionated man*. It seems there could be an 'opinionated man' in our earlier sense who not only jumps to conclusions upon being queried but manages to do so on the basis of simultaneously trumped-up reasons.

(One might try to block this by requiring that the reasons themselves have been occurrently or tacitly stored all along, but such a condition either (respectively) collapses the present account into the extrapolator theory again or launches a regress of tacit beliefs that seems to me vicious.)

(4) *The excited raconteur*. He is regaling his dinner companions with a voluble account of some startling incident, waving his arms and talking much too loudly. If he were simply to entertain the proposition that he was talking too loudly, he would instantly realize (and judge) that it was true. But not having entertained that proposition, he does not already know or believe it in any sense. (This case is due to Audi (1982).)

No further proposals, or at least no very plausible ones, occur to me; so I think it is time we considered abandoning the pursuit of a realistic notion of tacit belief. That leaves us with two options: to abandon tacit belief entirely, and maintain, contrary to common sense, that there is no such thing at all,[14] or to adopt some

[14] D. M. Armstrong has advocated this option in conversation. It has made its way into print just once that I know of:

'It is . . . clearly necessary that any proposition which someone is to believe should be, at least at some time and in some guise, present to his consciousness: it must, as the jargon had it, be entertained.' (Mayo (1967), p. 147).

instrumentalistic or otherwise deflationary account of the truth of ascriptions of tacit belief. Which is preferable?

8. INSTRUMENTALISM VERSUS ELIMINATION

There is a good deal to be said in favour of the instrumentalist approach. Other things being equal, we would prefer not to trample on common sense if a plausible instrumentalistic interpretation of tacit-belief ascription could be found. And there are contenders available: Field's option as discussed in section 5 above, for one, and, for another, Dennett's theory (1971, 1981*a*, 1981*b*, 1981*c*) according to which (very crudely) a creature believes that *P* provided the creature *ought* to believe that *P*, given the way it is situated in its environment, and one can achieve predictive success by attributing that belief accordingly.[15] (The apparent circularity here is to be removed, Dennett says, by specifying the interpretative strategy we are to use in making our attributions and the system of epistemic norms which it ineliminably involves ((1981*b*), p. 59; cf. (1981*c*), pp. 57–60).) Of the two, I incline toward Dennett's proposal, since it shows some promise of avoiding the relativity incurred by Field as remarked on above; even if common sense really treats tacit belief instrumentalistically, I do not see that it allows for the particular kind of relativity induced by Field's notion of obviousness.

A second reason for preferring instrumentalism to elimination is that it is still officially an open question whether there are any occurrent beliefs in the sense laid down in section 2 above.[16] If so

---

[15] e.g., any creature ought to form correct perceptual beliefs concerning the objects immediately confronting it, and ought to believe all the logical consequences of those beliefs, and ought to draw all the inductive inferences warranted probabilistically by them, and so on. In so far as real organisms fall short of this ideal of rationality, they fall short of being true believers, according to Dennett. The reason that belief ascription works as well as it does, and the reason that organisms live up the norms of rationality as well as they do, and hence count to some degree as believers, is that they are the products of *good design* on Mother Nature's part via the process of natural selection. (On which, see Lycan (1985*b*) and Stich (1985).)

[16] Harman (1978) emphasizes this and waxes pessimistic. Dennett (1975, 1981*b*) also expresses the gravest doubts, and makes the worthwhile point ((1981*b*), p. 49) that even if there is explicit representation in the human brain, ' . . . there is no reason to suppose the core *elements*, the concrete, salient, separately stored representation-tokens (and there must be some such elements in any complex information-processing system), will explicitly represent (or *be*) a subset of our *beliefs* at all. That is, if you were to sit down and write out a list of a thousand or so of your paradigmatic beliefs, *all* of them could turn out to be virtual, only implicitly

and if (we suppose) there simply are no tacit beliefs, then it is an *a fortiori* open question whether or not there are any beliefs at all—whether anyone has ever in fact believed anything—and this openness is an even more crass affront to common sense than is the elimination of tacit belief in and of itself. Nor is common sense all that is at stake. It seems to me that anything that is *judged* is belief, even though beliefs differ in categorial status from judgements, and it would take a lot to convince me that no one has ever judged.[17]

Finally, instrumentalism leaves open the possibility of an explanatory role for beliefs to play. As I have noted in section 4 above, we think that people make the judgements they do in many cases because hitherto tacit beliefs have been brought to their minds. Moreover, ascriptions of tacit belief warrant behavioural predictions just as securely as do ascriptions of occurrent belief; if you ask Mary whether she is as tall as eighteen feet, you will receive (in addition to a very peculiar look) a clear, crisp 'No' in reply.[18]

It should be noted that the actual explanatory role of tacit beliefs is not so clear as the foregoing remarks suggest, particularly if we have self-consciously eschewed a realistic treatment of such beliefs. The proximate cause of a judgement is either the accessing of an occurrent belief (in the actual-storage sense) or the searching of some other kind of information store, perhaps unknown to common sense, at the instigation of the relevant stimulus. If any such type of storage were taken as the categorical basis of a dispositional tacit belief realistically understood, then it would be natural to cite such a tacit belief as a cause of the judgement; but we are *not* now understanding 'tacit belief' realistically. If we understand our ascriptions of tacit beliefs, rather, as expressing just subjective measures of obviousness, on Field's theory, or our normative

stored or represented, and what was explicitly stored would be information (e.g., about memory addresses, procedures for problem-solving, or recognition, etc.) that was entirely unfamiliar.' However, as against this, it would be very surprising if judgements, inner tokenings, were *never* the results of assessing stored representations having the same semantic features.

[17] Perhaps there is a notion intermediate between judgement and occurrent belief, in my sense of 'stored-in long-term memory', that would serve. For example, let a 'super-occurrent' belief be the holding of a judgement in short-term memory. Being in a state of belief might be like sitting and hearing the reverberation of your judgement just before it fades from the specious present. If something like this can be made plausible in the face of, e.g., Wittgensteinian criticism, then I would be happy to eliminate the tacit beliefs.

[18] These points have been emphasized to me by Robert Matthews, Bas van Fraassen, and Mike Meyer.

opinions in regard to rationality, on Dennett's theory, they do not seem to be causal hypotheses at all. Indeed, the idea that tacit beliefs figure in the 'executive order of nature' is an *obstacle* to instrumentalism, not an advantage that instrumentalism has over elimination. It pushes rather against both, back in the direction of a realistic account, if only a plausible one could be found.

One might cite tacit beliefs as causes of nonverbal behaviour, bypassing occurrent belief and judgement entirely. For example, it is not unnatural to suggest that among the causes of my having sat down in this chair was my tacit belief that it would hold me. Not unnatural, perhaps, but not obvious either, particularly (again) on an instrumentalistic understanding of tacit belief. The underlying intuition seems to be that I would not have sat down if I had not believed that the chair would hold me. But this counterfactual's antecedent is ambiguous between 'If I had not held the (tacit) belief that the chair would hold me' and 'If I had held the belief that the chair would not hold me'. On the former reading, the counterfactual seems to me no more obvious than the causal thesis itself, while, on the latter, it simply does not support the causal thesis at all. As before, the causal thesis pushes towards realism rather than towards instrumentalism as against elimination; and in the case of non-verbal as opposed to verbal behaviour it is not so obvious that common sense ascribes a causal role to tacit belief in any case.

But it may still be true that tacit beliefs play an *explanatory* role, since not all explanation is causal explanation. Sometimes we explain (albeit shallowly) by merely putting the *explanandum* in context, by subsuming it under a particularly illuminating generalization or classifying it in an unforeseen way. (Humeans and positivists tend to think that all explanation is of this nature.) Sometimes to explain is to rationalize or to vindicate, to show that the *explanandum* is a good thing in some sense. If Dennett's instrumentalism is a correct account of belief ascription, then explanation of behaviour by reference to beliefs and desires is of this rationalizing sort. Thus, the instrumentalist can at least explain away the intuition that beliefs are causes, and still has the advantage over the eliminativist of preserving their weaker, explanatory role.[19]

---

[19] However, see P. M. Churchland's (1970) criticism of W. Dray's version of this view. Churchland points out in particular that attitude ascriptions figure as the antecedents of subjunctive conditionals concerning behaviour, which is hard to explain on the present version of instrumentalism.

9. EPILOGUE

A few sources of dissatisfaction remain. First, there is as yet no *well worked out* and defended version of instrumentalism available; Dennett's view, in particular, has been criticized vigorously and with effect in the literature.[20] Second, the bifurcation of belief into kinds, one treated realistically and the other instrumentalistically, is regrettable. The occurrent/tacit distinction is drawn by common sense, to be sure, but if we take our Sellarsian representationalist theory of occurrent belief seriously not just as metaphysics but as a semantic theory of belief-sentences (Lycan (1981), (1985a)), we shall probably have to concede that the belief predicate is at best paronymous between occurrent-belief and tacit-belief ascriptions. For surely neither the presumably functional relation that an occurrent believer bears to his or her stored representation nor the derived relation that the believer bears to the complement of our belief-sentence is the same relation as that which a tacit believer (instrumentalistically construed) bears to the complement clause, if any.[21] This lexical ambiguity is unpalatable.

Third, it seems to me that even tacit belief requires some real executive goings-on in nature: conceptual preparation, for one; just as a subject cannot occurrently believe that X is F without having the concepts of X-hood and F-ness, it seems wrong to ascribe tacit belief to such a person either. Mary could not even tacitly believe that our daughter's Sunday dress had not been zipprodted if she did not know what zipprodting was.[22] An instrumentalist might get round this point by providing an instrumentalistic account of concept possession—concepts are only abilities, after all. But it seems the *intentionality* of tacit beliefs also requires the usual apparatus of causal chains. If no inner state of Mary is causally

[20] See, e.g., Stich (1981), Richardson (1980), and Bechtel (1982).

[21] What relation this is taken to be depends on the specific version of instrumentalism in hand. Most versions seem to me to make a mystery of the semantics of belief-sentences, and to make it puzzling why belief-sentence complements are, in Sellars's phrase, 'sentences used in a special way'. In Lycan (1981), p. 143, I have accused Dennett in particular of this fault, but falsely, for I now see the germ of a Dennettian explanation of Sellars's datum: beliefs are identified by sentential complements because it is on sentences that the epistemic norms of logic and probability theory are defined and it is these normative sciences that (according to Dennett) make beliefs beliefs. Sentential complements mark points in epistemic-normative space.

[22] No, sorry, my lips are sealed.

grounded in the city of Stockholm, she cannot correctly be said to have even a tacit belief *about* Stockholm. Any instrumentalist theory will have to take account of this, and any theory that does will be beginning, at least, to edge towards realism.[23] (Here again, there is no comfort for the eliminativist unless realism has been utterly written off.)

The situation is very unsatisfactory. Realism, instrumentalism, and eliminativism concerning tacit belief are all unpromising, yet they seem to be the only choices. Only the devising of a new realist analysis or the working out of an instrumentalistic one will settle the matter. Until then, Mary will have to keep her thoughts about my tie freshly occurrent, if she wants me to do anything about them. I shall never give in, anyway.[24]

BIBLIOGRAPHY

Armstrong, D. M. (1973) *Belief, Truth and Knowledge* (Cambridge UP).

Audi, R. (1982) 'Believing and Affirming', *Mind*, 91.

Bechtel, P. W. (1982) 'Realism, Instrumentalism, and the Intentional Stance' (unpublished MS).

Block, N. J. (1981) 'Psychologism and Behaviorism', *Philosophical Review*, 90.

Boër, S. and Lycan, W. G. (1986) 'Castañeda's Theory of Knowing', in J. Tomberlin (ed.), *Profiles: Hector-Neri Castañeda* (Dordrecht).

Castañeda, H.-N. (1980) 'The Theory of Questions, Epistemic Powers, and the Indexical Theory of Knowledge, in P. French, T. Uehling, and H. Wettstein (edd.), *Midwest Studies in Philosophy*, Vol. 5 (University of Minn. Press).

Churchland, P. M. (1970) 'The Logical Character of Action Explanations', *Philosophical Review*, 79.

Dennett, D. C. (1971) 'Intentional Systems', *Journal of Philosophy*, 68; reprinted in Dennett (1978).

—— (1975), 'Brain Writing and Mind Reading', in K. Gunderson (ed.),

---

[23] Dennett can probably deal with this difficulty by invoking (*a*) the causal ancestries of the 'core elements' he mentions in the passage quoted in n. 16 above, and (*b*) the environmental source of the perceptual beliefs that initiate for him the whole business of belief ascription.

[24] In addition to the friends and colleagues mentioned in preceding footnotes, I must thank Lynne Baker, Paul Churchland, Dan Dennett, Michael Devitt, Pat Manfredi, and Robert Richardson for extensive and illuminating correspondence on this topic. I am also grateful to the students in my 1982 seminars at the Ohio State University and the University of North Carolina, particularly Lisa Kearns and Mike Meyer, for their very helpful discussion.

Minnesota Studies in the Philosophy of Science, Vol. 7 (University of Minn. Press), reprinted in Dennett (1978).

—— (1978) *Brainstorms* (Montgomery, Vt.).

—— (1981*a*) 'Making Sense of Ourselves', *Philosophical Topics*, 12.

—— (1981*b*) 'Three Kinds of Intentional Psychology', in R. A. Healey (ed.), *Reduction, Time and Reality* (Cambridge UP).

—— (1981*c*) 'True Believers: The Intentional Strategy and Why it Works', in A. F. Heath (ed.), *Scientific Explanation* (Oxford UP).

—— (1983) 'Cognitive Wheels: The Frame Problem in AI' (unpublished MS).

de Sousa, R. (1971) 'How to Give a Piece of Your Mind', *Review of Metaphysics*, 25.

Dreyfus, H. (1979) *What Computers Can't Do* (revised ed., New York).

Fahlman, S. E. (1979) 'Representing and Using Real-World Knowledge', in P. H. Winston and R. H. Brown (edd.), *Artificial Intelligence: An MIT Perspective* (MIT Press).

Field, H. (1978) 'Mental Representation', *Erkenntnis*, 13.

Fodor, J. A. (1981) 'Three Cheers for Propositional Attitudes', in *RePresentations* (MIT Press).

Foley, R. (1978) 'Inferential Justification and the Infinite Regress', *American Philosophical Quarterly*, 15.

Harman, G. (1970) 'Knowledge, Reasons, and Causes', *Journal of Philosophy*, 67.

—— (1978) 'Is There Mental Representation?' in W. Savage (ed.), *Minnesota Studies in the Philosophy of Science*, Vol. 9 (University of Minn. Press).

Hunter, J. F. M. (1980) 'Believing', in *Midwest Studies in Philosophy*, Vol. 5.

Kripke, S. A. (1982) *Wittgenstein on Rules and Private Language* (Harvard UP).

Lehnert, W. (1979) 'Representing Physical Objects in Memory', in M. Ringle (ed.), *Philosophical Perspectives in Artificial Intelligence* (Brighton).

Lehrer, K. (1974) *Knowledge* (Oxford UP).

Levi, I., and Morgenbesser, S. (1964) 'Belief and Disposition', *American Philosophical Quarterly*, 1.

Lycan, W. G. (1981) 'Toward a Homuncular Theory of Believing', *Cognition and Brain Theory*, 4.

—— (1985*a*) 'The Paradox of Naming', in B. K. Matilal and J. L. Shaw (edd.), *Analytical Philosophy in Comparative Perspective* (Dordrecht).

—— (1985*b*) 'Epistemic Value', *Synthese*, 64.

Mayo, B. (1967) 'Belief and Constraint', in A. P. Griffiths (ed.), *Knowledge and Belief* (Oxford UP).

Minsky, M. (1975) 'A Framework for Representing Knowledge', P. H. Winston (ed.), *The Psychology of Computer Vision* (New York).

Moore, J., and Newell, A. (1974) 'How Can MERLIN Understand?' in L. Gregg (ed.), *Knowledge and Cognition* (Potomac, Md.).

Nisbett, R., and Ross, L. (1980) *Human Inference: Strategies and Shortcomings of Social Judgment* (Englewood Cliffs, NJ).

Pappas, G. (1981) 'Basing Relations', in Pappas (ed.), *Justification and Knowledge* (Dordrecht).

Powers, L. H. (1978) 'Knowledge by Deduction', *Philosophical Review*, 87.

Pylyshyn, Z. (1979) 'Complexity and the Study of Artificial and Human Intelligence', in M. Ringle (ed.), *Philosophical Perspectives in Artificial Intelligence* (Brighton).

Ramsey, F. P. (1926) 'Truth and Probability', reprinted in D. H. Mellor (ed.), *Foundations* (Atlantic Highlands, NJ).

Richardson, R. (1980) 'Intentional Realism or Intentional Instrumentalism?', *Cognition and Brain Theory*, 3.

—— (1981) 'Internal Representation: Prologue to a Theory of Intentionality', *Philosophical Topics*, 12.

Rosch, E. (1977) 'Human Categorization', in N. Warren (ed.), *Advances in Cross-Cultural Psychology*, Vol. 1 (London).

Schank, R. C., and Abelson, R. P. (1977) *Scripts, Plans, Goals and Understanding* (Hillsdale, NJ).

Sellars, W. F. (1956) 'Empiricism and the Philosophy of Mind', in H. Feigl and M. Scriven (edd.), *Minnesota Studies in the Philosophy of Science*, Vol. 1 (University of Minn. Press); reprinted in *Science, Perception and Reality* (London, 1963).

—— (1958) contribution to the 'Chisholm–Sellars Correspondence on Intentionality' (3 August 1956) in H. Feigl, M. Scriven and G. Maxwell (edd.), *Minnesota Studies in the Philosophy of Science*, Vol. 2 (University of Minn. Press); reprinted in A. Marras (ed.), *Intentionality, Mind, and Language* (University of Illinois Press, 1972).

—— (1967) *Science and Metaphysics* (London).

—— (1969) 'Language as Thought and as Communication', *Philosophy and Phenomenological Research*, 29.

Stich, S. P. (1981) 'Dennett on Intentional Systems', *Philosophical Topics*, 12.

—— (1985) 'Could Man Be an Irrational Animal?' *Synthese*, 64.

Swain, M. (1981a) 'Justification and the Basis of Belief', in G. Pappas (ed.), *Justification and Knowledge* (Dordrecht).

—— (1981b) *Reasons and Knowledge* (Cornell UP).

Tolliver, J. T. (1980) *Reasons, Perception, and Information* (Ohio State University doctoral dissertation).

Vendler, Z. (1972) *Res Cogitans* (Cornell UP).

Vickers, J. (1969) 'Judgment and Belief', in K. Y. Lambert (ed.), *The Logical Way of Doing Things* (Yale UP).

Winograd, T. (1975) 'Frame Representations and the Declarative–Procedural Controversy', in D. Bobrow and A. Collins (edd.), *Representation and Understanding* (New York).

—— (1976) 'Towards a Procedural Understanding of Semantics', *Revue internationale de philosophie*, 117–118.

—— and Bobrow, D. G. 1977 'An Overview of KRL, a Knowledge Representation Language', *Cognitive Science*, 1.

CHAPTER 5

THE REAL TROUBLE WITH PROPOSITIONS*

STEPHEN SCHIFFER

I. INTRODUCTION

For a long time I believed that if there were propositions they were ideally suited to be the objects of propositional attitudes. I thought that the only serious problem unique to the propositional theory of propositional attitudes was that, being creatures of darkness, propositions were hard to believe in. I now realize that I was wrong: the real trouble with propositions is that, even granted that they exist, propositional attitudes cannot be relations to them.

There is, I believe, more than one way of constructing an argument against the theory that believing is a relation to propositions, and this should not be surprising if that theory is indeed false; but this essay is concerned with only one of those ways.[1] I shall argue that the propositional theory founders on beliefs involving natural-kind concepts. First, however, there are some preliminary points to be made by way of cleaning up the area of the argument.

(1) The theory in question is that propositional attitudes are relations to propositions. To say that believing (which will serve as my exemplar) is a relation to a proposition is to say two things. First, that the letter 'p' in the schema

x believes p

is a genuine objectual variable; and second, that propositions are the values of that variable. Propositions are abstract, objective,

---

* © Stephen Schiffer 1986.

[1] One other way concerns the problem of specifying modes of presentation to enter into *de re* beliefs about physical objects (see n. 16 below). A second way concerns the infamous, but not well enough appreciated, Paradox of Analysis, while a third, and somewhat related, way exploits an argument in Burge (1978) to show that the principles that correctly describe substitution in belief contexts are not consistent with *any* propositionalist theory of belief.

language-independent entities that have essentially the truth conditions they have.

They are abstract in that they are not in space or time: the proposition that snow is white is not anywhere, and, while it really exists, there is no time at which it began to exist and none at which it will cease to exist. The abstractness of propositions does not, however, preclude them from having concrete particulars as constituents—the Empire State Building, according to certain propositionalists, is a constituent of the proposition expressed by 'The Empire State Building is in Tacoma, Washington'.

They are objective in contrast to the subjectivity of pains and mental images, which can have no existence apart from the minds which have them. Propositions are not mental entities, and would have existed even if there had never been people to conceive them.

They have their truth conditions essentially, in contrast to the contingent way in which sentences and other representations have them. It is a contingent fact, and so might well have been otherwise, that the sequence of marks 'snow is white' is true if and only if snow is white, but the proposition that snow is white has that truth condition in every possible world.

Perhaps the language-independence of propositions is their most important feature. For the propositionalist, the proposition that snow is white is as ontologically and conceptually distinct from the *sentence* 'snow is white' as Carlos Lopes is from the name 'Carlos Lopes'; a proposition, Frege wrote, 'is like a planet which, already before anyone has seen it, has been in interaction with other planets', and 'when one apprehends or thinks a [proposition] one does not create it but only comes to stand in a certain relation . . . to what already existed beforehand'.[2] The importance of this independence is, of course, that if it were not the case, one could not explain the meaning of 'snow is white' in terms of its standing in a certain contingent relation to the proposition that snow is white; and if one could not do that one would be without motivation for being a propositionalist with respect to propositional attitudes. For anyone who subscribes to the Gricean programme of intention-based semantics, which seeks to explain the content of marks and sounds in terms of the content of mental states, this is especially so.

Most of what can be said of propositions can also be said of the

---

[2] Frege (1967), pp. 29–30. Frege's word for proposition was 'thought'.

properties and relations that help to compose them. They, too, for the propositionalist, are abstract, objective, and, especially, language-independent. There is no objective and language-independent proposition to be expressed by 'snow is white' unless there is an objective and language-independent property of whiteness to be expressed by 'white'. The ontological commitment to propositions carries with it a general commitment to Platonic realism, which is why, of course, so many people object to it. One reason I am emphasizing the language-independence of propositions and properties is that unless it is kept in mind, propositions are apt to seem more readily available than they may in fact be. The problem is that there is a risk that a certain *pleonastic* use of 'property' will precipitately seduce one into thinking that language-independent properties, and thus the propositions they determine, exist. Suppose, to approach what I mean, one were concerned to construct a correspondence theory that required that there were *facts* that were language-independent in just the way that propositions are supposed to be. Then one would take no comfort in the utterly pleonastic sense of 'fact' that enabled one to move back and forth between 'Michele is funny' and 'It is a fact that Michele is funny'. Likewise, if one's concern were the existence of *language-independent* properties, one would take no comfort in the pleonastic sense of 'property' that enabled one to move back and forth between 'Michele is funny' and 'Michele has the property of being funny'. The full import of these remarks will be made manifest later, when they are put to use; in the meantime I should reiterate that in making my *primary* objection to the propositional theory of propositional attitudes I shall not be taking issue on the existence of propositions. However, I shall express doubt about the existence of certain non-pleonastic properties, and thereby give voice to a further reason for doubting the propositional theory. The case against that theory may well be overdetermined.

(2) Different sorts of things can count as propositions in the sense glossed—functions from possible worlds into truth values, or fine-grained complexes containing individuals and properties, such as the situation-types of Barwise and Perry.[3] I shall not be an interloper in this family affair; my intention is to raise a problem for the propositional theory of propositional attitudes, whatever kind of

[3] Barwise and Perry (1983). See also Adams (1974), Bealer (1982), Lewis (1972), Loar (1981), and Plantinga (1974).

proposition is involved. I shall, however, in the ensuing discussion, avail myself of a certain simplifying assumption.

Suppose that

(*a*) Ralph believes that snow is white,

and that two propositionalists agree that this may be represented as

(*b*) B (Ralph, the proposition that snow is white).[4]

Then, even if they disagree about what sort of thing that proposition is, they will at least agree that the expression 'that snow is white' functions in (*a*) as a complex singular term which refers to that proposition, and that the reference of that singular term is determined by the references of its semantically relevant parts. Perhaps 'snow' there refers to the stuff snow, 'is white' to the property of being white, and the proposition thus determined is one that, necessarily, is true just in case snow is white. Still, the two theorists may at this juncture differ over whether or not the proposition *contains* those referents as *constituents*. If propositions are taken to be functions from possible worlds into truth values, then they do not contain the entities that determine them. Our mooted proposition would not be a complex containing snow and the property of being white, but, say, that partial function which maps a possible world *w* onto truth iff snow exists and is white in *w*, onto falsity iff snow exists and is not white in *w*, and is undefined otherwise. Notoriously, this conception of unstructured propositions may seem ill suited to provide the objects of belief, for it entails that necessarily equivalent propositions are identical, and that, therefore, one believes all mathematical and logical truths if one believes any, there being only one to begin with. For this reason, and some others, other theorists, seeking more finely individuated entities, construe propositions as structured entities the constituents of which are the objects, properties, operators, etc. which determine them. Although it will soon be evident that structured propositions stand a better chance of surviving the argument I shall aim at all propositions, I do not, as I have said, wish to take sides in intra-propositionalist disputes. However, for expository reasons I propose harmlessly to *represent* propositions, of whatever stripe, as ordered *n*-tuples of the things which

---

[4] As we shall presently see, the propositionalist is not committed to representing (*a*) as (*b*).

determine them. Thus, if in (*a*) 'snow' refers to snow, and 'is white' to the property of being white, then I would represent the proposition referred to in (*a*) and (*b*) as the ordered pair

(*c*) ⟨snow, the property of being white⟩.

The possible-worlds theorist obviously cannot identify his proposition with this ordered pair, and the advocate of structured propositions may well wish to treat his complexes as irreducible entities, not definable in terms of any set-theoretic apparatus. But neither should object to our style of representation: the possible-worlds theorist can construe (*c*) as representing the function it determines, and the threorist of fine-grained propositions can construe (*c*) as standing in for his irreducible complex, which has just the same constituents as our ordered pair. And in the same unpolemical vein, I shall allow myself to speak of the constituents of propositions, rather than speaking periphrastically of the constituents of the ordered *n*-tuple which represents the proposition in question.

(3) The theory in question holds that 'believes' in sentences of the form '*x* believes that σ' expresses a relation which relates believers to propositions. This, however, does not entail that substitution-instances of 'that σ' *must* refer to propositions. Thus consider an utterance of

(*i*) Henry believes that that girl is clever.

A propositionalist might, consistently with his being a propositionalist, hold that the occurrence of 'that girl' refers to a certain girl, and that the occurrence of 'is clever' refers to the property of being clever, but deny that the occurrence of 'that that girl is clever' refers to the proposition ⟨that girl, cleverness⟩, and thus deny that (*i*) is representable as

B (Henry, ⟨that girl, cleverness⟩).

He might—still consistently with his propositionalism—hold that the correct representation of (*i*) is

(*ii*) (E*m*) (*m* is a mode of presentation of that girl & B (Henry, ⟨*m*, cleverness⟩)).

This does not tell us what proposition Henry believes, but merely that he believes *some* proposition which contains *some* mode of presentation of the girl in question. On this way of representing (*i*), the 'that'-clause in (*i*), 'that that girl is clever', does not refer to what Henry believes, but rather provides an indirect and partial characterization of that proposition, if any, believing which makes (*i*) true, if it is true.

The representation of (*i*) as (*ii*) is, of course, a familiar propositionalist move. What we must next note is that it is equally *consistent* with the propositional theory to represent (*i*) as

> (Em) (m is a mode of presentation of cleverness & B (Henry, $\langle$that girl, m $\rangle$))

(or as

> (Em) (Em') (m is a mode of presentation of that girl, m' of cleverness & B (Henry, $\langle m, m' \rangle$))

—I am now unconcerned with the role in (*i*) of 'that girl'). This is not a familiar propositionalist move, and I think for good reason; but the issues that are about to confront us require that we see it as a possible move, one available to the propositionalist.

2. THE STRUCTURE OF THE ARGUMENT

Toby is known to have a pet named 'Gustav', and Tanya, to relieve curiosity about the kind of animal Gustav is, says,

> (1) Gustav is a dog,

thereby revealing that

> (2) Tanya believes that Gustav is a dog.

If the theory that believing is a relation to a proposition is true, then there is some proposition p that is the content of the belief expressed by Tanya when she uttered (1), and it is the fact of Tanya's believing p, perhaps together with some other fact, that makes (2) true. My objection to this theory is that it cannot be right because there is no plausible account of the proposition that is supposed to be the content of Tanya's belief, and this because there is no plausible account of the role that 'dog' plays in (2) in the determination of that proposition.

Our question is to be the contribution which 'dog' makes to the content of Tanya's belief. Happily, therefore, we may ignore for a while the vagaries of the so-called *de re/de dicto* distinction as regards singular terms, and harmlessly pretend that the only semantically relevant role of the name 'Gustav' in (2) is to refer to the creature Gustav and introduce him directly into the proposition that is the content of Tanya's belief that Gustav is a dog. So, relative to this simplifying assumption, the proposition that provides the complete content of Tanya's belief is some completion of the proposition

$$\langle \text{Gustav}, ? \rangle,$$

and the question confronting the propositionalist is just this: what is to take place of *?* ? That is, *what proposition* is (relative to the simplifying assumption) the content of Tanya's belief?

There are two possible answers available to the propositionalist, and they are, I believe, mutually exclusive and jointly exhaustive of the answers available to him.

First, he may hold that the proposition which provides the complete content of Tanya's belief is (given the simplifying assumption about 'Gustav') the proposition

(3) $\langle \text{Gustav, the property of being a dog} \rangle$,

which proposition is true in any given possible world just in ease Gustav is in that world a dog. On this view the correct representation of (2) would be

(4) B (Tanya, $\langle \text{Gustav, doghood} \rangle$).

This would be the natural position to take if one thought that the 'that'-clause in (2), 'that Gustav is a dog', was a singular term which referred to what Tanya believed, (2) thus enjoying the representation.

B (Tanya, the proposition that Gustav is a dog).

For the belief ascribed to Tanya is, evidently, one that is true in any given possible world just in case Gustav has in that world the property of being a dog. I shall call this answer to our question— that (3) is the content of Tanya's belief—the *classical* propositional position; basically, it is the position that predicates in 'that'-clauses simply refer to the properties and relations they express and introduce them directly into the propositions believed.

Second, the propositionalist may hold, refinements apart, that the proposition which provides the complete content of Tanya's belief contains not doghood, but a *mode of presentation* of it. This line is, we shall see, best thought of as developing out of the failure of the classical response, and it takes its cue from a familiar Fregean way of treating beliefs that are *de re* with respect to ordinary physical objects. Someone taking this line would want to deny that the 'that'-clause in (2) referred to the complete content of Tanya's belief. He would want to say that (2) would be best represented as

(E*m*) (*m* is a mode of presentation of doghood & B (Tanya, ⟨Gustav, *m*⟩)).

In this way *different* propositions, containing *different* ways of thinking of doghood, different modes of presentation of it, can be the content of a belief ascribed by (2); (2) does not give the proposition believed, but only gives a partial characterization of it, as a proposition containing some mode of presentation of doghood. This line will be more fully motivated and carefully set up later, when the need for it arises.

My main objection to the classical theory, which I make in the next section, is that, given the only plausible account of what the property of being a dog might be, it is clear that (3) cannot be the content of Tanya's belief.

My main argument against the mode-of-presentation account, which I develop in sections 4 to 7, has two parts. First, I argue that there are quite general difficulties in the way of developing a mode-of-presentation treatment of (2) that are independent of any specific proposal about what the mode of presentation in a case such as Tanya's might be; then I argue that there are difficulties facing each of the candidate answers to the question of what those modes of presentation of doghood might be.

A further objection whose validity would sink any propositional-ist account of beliefs involving the concept *dog* is briefly entertained near the close of this essay, when I suggest that there might not be a genuinely non-pleonastic, language-independent property of being a dog.

3. THE CLASSICAL THEORY: ⟨GUSTAV, DOGHOOD⟩ AS THE CONTENT OF THE BELIEF THAT GUSTAV IS A DOG

The proposal before us, the classical theory of Tanya's belief, holds that the complete content of her belief that Gustav is a dog is the proposition (3) ⟨Gustav, doghood⟩, relative, of course, to our simplifying assumption about 'Gustav', which I shall not continue to mention. But I think that we can show that this cannot be right once we see what property the property of being a dog would be, if there really is a genuinely language-independent, non-pleonastic property of being a dog.

The classical theory has it that the sole function of 'is a dog' in (2), 'Tanya believes that Gustav is a dog', is to introduce doghood into that proposition that is the content of the belief that Gustav is a dog. The question now to be addressed is: exactly what property is this property of being a dog? Of course, one possible response to this question is to reject it, protesting that the property of being a dog is primitive and irreducible; it cannot be specified in any other terms: it is the property of being a dog, and there is an end to it. This has not in fact been a line advocated or implied by any historical personage, and we would be well advised to consider it later, after more familiar lines have been exhausted.

It is not, we shall soon see, at all plausible to think that doghood is primitive and irreducible; hence, if there is such a property, it is one specifiable in other terms, without using the word 'dog'. What might this other way of specifying the property be? One venerable answer, hobbled by Wittgenstein, demolished by Kripke and Putnam,[5] is that 'dog' is somehow definable in terms of those more or less observable properties by which, in a paradigm observational case, one identifies a thing as a dog. It is in fact difficult to construct a verbal definition of 'dog' along these lines, for we lack neat expressions for ascribing the doggy appearance and demeanour; but it is more or less clear what the intended properties are. Nor is it hard to fathom the appeal which this account has for the theorist who would represent (2) as (4): they are properties by which we identify a thing as a dog, and their possession by a creature does not seem to be merely evidence or a symptom of its having the further property of being a dog; most importantly, they, if any, are properties with which, in Russell's sense, we are 'acquainted',[6] which makes them eminently suitable as constituents of belief contents.

Nevertheless, these properties are neither separately necessary nor jointly sufficient for being a dog. None of them is necessary, for

[5] Wittgenstein (1958); Kripke (1980); Putnam (1975).
[6] Russell (1959).

we can imagine a creature which looked and behaved quite unlike a dog, but which we classed as one anyway because it was the offspring of paradigm dogs and was relevantly like them genetically; or, to echo Kripke, we might learn that, owing to certain optical distortions, dogs did not really have the doggy appearance which, under the illusive conditions, we took them to have. And the conjunction of these observational properties fails to provide a sufficient condition for being a dog, for, as Kripke and Putnam have taught us, we can easily imagine a thing of another species (a reptile, say), or of no recognizable biological species at all, having just the appearance and demeanour of paradigm dogs, and this thing would not be a dog.

Many philosophers have joined Kripke and Putnam in taking such counter-examples to show that, for any possible world w, a thing is a dog in w just in case it belongs in w to the natural kind to which in the actual world all and only dogs belong. This natural kind, if it exists, is reasonably taken to be the species, *Canis familiaris*, to which dogs in the actual world belong. It is as if the word 'dog' got introduced as a rigid designator of the species, its reference fixed by the description 'the species of those things', where 'those things' referred to some privileged sample of the things we call 'dog'.

If this is correct, then the property of being a dog is the property of belonging to *Canis familiaris*, and (3) is now revealed to be

(5) ⟨ ⟨Gustav,   *Canis   familiaris*⟩,   the   kind-membership relation⟩,

which proposition is true in any given possible world just in case in that world Gustav belongs to the species, *Canis familiaris*, to which all dogs in *the actual world* belong.[7]

Even this will admit of further reduction, if there really is the species *Canis familiaris*; that is, if dogs really do constitute a natural kind. It seems reasonable to suppose that membership of the species is itself to be determined by a certain empirically discoverable internal structure; that is, most plausibly, a certain complex genetic property, a genotype common to all and only dogs.[8] Whether or not the natural kind is to be individuated wholly in terms of genetic

[7] Cf. Salmon (1981), pp. 42–76.
[8] I am skirting issues in the philosophy of biology; not all biologists would agree that zoological species are constituted by genotypes. But that does seem to be the only view consonant with the Kripke–Putnam gloss that natural kinds are constituted

properties does not really matter for our purposes. What does matter is that the natural kind, the abstract entity *Canis familiaris*, if it exists, is not anything with which we are directly acquainted. It remains to be discovered by science what that natural kind is; at present we only have, so to say, 'knowledge by description' of the kind, as the natural kind, whatever it turns out to be, to which paradigm dogs belong. What we do not have at present is knowledge of the internal properties that constitute, or define, the species.

Let us suppose that there really is a definite abstract entity that is the species, the natural kind, to which all and only dogs belong, and that '*Canis familiaris*' names it, thus removing any doubt about the *existence* of the proposition (5) ⟨ ⟨Gustav, *Canis familiaris*⟩, the kind-membership relation⟩. None the less, we cannot plausibly suppose that (5) is the complete content of Tanya's belief. For suppose that we came across a race of dogs whom we mistakenly supposed not to be dogs, and, in our ignorance, decided that 'shmog' would stand for any creature of the same biologial species as those creatures. In that event, (2) could be true while

(6) Tanya believes that Gustav is a shmog

was false: Tanya, like us, may fail to believe that shmogs are dogs. But if the content sentence in (2) refers to (5), then so must the one in (6).

We do not need shmogs to make the point. Suppose that scientists discovered that a certain complex genotype, G, was in fact constitutive of the species of dogs. G would, of course, be a property that enjoyed an intrinsic description couched wholly in biochemical terms, daunting words like 'nucleotide', 'deoxyribose' and 'adenine'. Now Tanya might, in principle, be acquainted with G under its biochemical description, know that it was constitutive of some natural kind, but not know that that natural kind was the species of dogs. She might say, 'There is some natural kind constituted by G, and I hereby rigidly designate that natural kind "Oscar".' Then it might further happen that, as regards a certain creature, Lulu,

(7) Tanya believes that Lulu belongs to Oscar

was true, while it was not true that

by 'internal' properties that account for certain observable similarities among members of the kind.

(8) Tanya believes that Lulu is a dog.

This might be the case if Tanya's acquaintance with Lulu was limited to a microscopic examination of certain of her cells. But if (5) were the complete content of Tanya's belief that Gustav is a dog, then, by parity of reasoning, it would also have to be held that (7) and (8) were logically equivalent, 'believes' in both serving to relate Tanya to the proposition

$\langle$ $\langle$Lulu, *Canis familiaris* [= Oscar]$\rangle$, the kind-membership relation$\rangle$.

It seems clear that the complete content of the belief Tanya expresses when she says 'Lulu belongs to Oscar' is not the complete content of the belief which she would express were she then also to say 'Lulu is a dog'.

This is by no means to suggest that the species of dogs is not a constituent of the proposition believed when one has a belief whose content can be specified using the word 'dog'. But it does suggest that, if the natural kind does enter into those contents, it does so only under a mode of presentation that makes that content ascribable using 'dog'. This suggestion—that beliefs such as Tanya's are of natural kinds under modes of presentation—will presently be critically examined. Before that we must complete the case against the classical theory by considering the remaining possible way of holding it.[9]

---

[9] Why not dig in one's heels and insist that (2) and (6) *cannot* differ in truth value because the same proposition—viz., (5)—*is* referred to in both sentences (and likewise, *mutatis mutandis*, for (7) and (8))? True, someone holding this theory might concede, Tanya believes, or may believe, that Gustav is not a shmog; but that merely shows that she has inconsistent beliefs, not that (6) can be false when (2) is true. True, this theorist might concede, there is a strong intuition that these sentences can differ in truth value—as strong, to be sure, as the intuition which tells us that one might believe that Istanbul was Istanbul while failing to believe that Istanbul was Constantinople—but perhaps that can be accounted for by appeal to Tanya's metalinguistic beliefs, to the fact that she does not know that the sentences 'Gustav is a dog' and 'Gustav is a shmog' express the same proposition.

Now I do not see how one can consistently, or coherently, take this line about natural-kind terms in 'that'-clauses unless one is prepared to take what is *mutatis mutandis* the same line about singular terms in 'that'-clauses, and many believe that that application of the 'Fido'–Fido theory to belief contexts is a position which Frege refuted nearly a hundred years ago. And with good reason. For Ralph might point to a man in a photograph and speak the truth when he says,

(*i*) I believe that that man is senile.

I am thus led to conclude that (3), ⟨Gustav, doghood⟩, is not the content of Tanya's belief that Gustav is a dog, if doghood is not a primitive and irreducible property. For if there is a non-pleonastic property of being a dog, and it is identical to a property specifiable in other terms, then that property would most plausibly be the biological species, the natural kind, of dogs, and (3) would be (5); but, we have seen, (5) cannot be the content of Tanya's belief.

Therefore, (3) is the content of Tanya's belief only if doghood is primitive and irreducible. But this is why I think that, if there really is an objective, language-independent property of being a dog, it is not irreducible. Suppose that God were to tell you absolutely everything that could possibly be relevant to Gustav's being a dog, other than that Gustav had the property of being a dog, or other things trivially tantamount to that, such as that Gustav was of the same species as something which was a dog. God's description would apprize you of every morphological and behavioural, every phenotypic and genetic fact about Gustav; and it would tell you with what things, likewise described, he was conspecific, and from what

And he might further be speaking the truth when he then says,

(*ii*) I do not believe that I am senile,

even though, and alas, he is, unbeknown to himself, the man in the photograph.

But a theorist who would take the hard line on (2) and (6) must evidently deny this; he must insist, in conformity to his line on Tanya, that (*i*) and (*ii*) must differ in truth value, as (*i*) affirms, while (*ii*) denies, that Ralph is belief-related to the proposition ⟨Ralph, senility⟩. Ralph, this theorist must say, is unknowingly speaking falsely in uttering (*ii*); he really does believe himself to be senile. Of course, the theorist will add, Ralph might also believe himself not to be senile, but that, as in Tanya's case, merely shows that he has inconsistent beliefs, and not that (*ii*) is true.

It is by no means clear what could be thought to motivate this 'Fido'–Fido line about singular terms in belief contexts. Certainly it is not needed to hold a 'Fido'–Fido *semantics* for singular terms (see Schiffer (1981)). Certainly, too, the intuition that (*i*) and (*ii*) can both be true is very strong; so strong, in fact, that this sort of case would ordinarily be taken to be a knock-down counter-example to any 'Fido'–Fido theory which claimed that (*i*) and (*ii*) were contradictory utterances. Anyone who would maintain the 'Fido'–Fido doctrine in the face of such intuitions owes an explanation that would convincingly explain them away. But merely to mention the obvious fact that Ralph does not know that 'I' and 'that man' have the same reference does not even begin to explain anything. How could it: Ralph fails to think that they have the same reference precisely because he fails to believe that he is that man! (Likewise, Tanya fails to believe that 'dog' and 'shmog' denote the same creatures because she fails to believe that shmogs are dogs.) There is more that the 'Fido'–Fido theorist would have to explain. For example, how, on his view, is one to explain the fact that the utterances of (*i*) and (*ii*) do not convict Ralph of irrationality, although that is what he would be convicted of were he now to utter 'I don't believe that that man is senile' or 'I believe that I'm senile'?

things he had descended; it would even tell you that Gustav was of the same species as the such and such animals with respect to which the word 'dog' was first introduced. Now anyone who thinks that there really is a property of being a dog but denies that it is identifiable with any property specifiable in genetic (or other 'biological') terms, must insist that there is an entirely determinate and objective, but irreducible, property of being a dog such that the fact that Gustav has that property is an objective fact distinct from and over and above all of these other facts about him. Presumably one could know absolutely everything about Gustav without knowing, or even believing, that he had this further, irreducible property of being a dog. But *how*, if this is what being a dog really consists in, could one ever come to know or believe, after being graced with the God-given knowledge, that Gustav was a dog? The property of being a dog could not be an observable property; we know all of them. But then by what means could we apprehend, in the situation imagined, that Gustav had this irreducible property? Are we supposed to have some special faculty, akin perhaps to moral intuition, for discerning it? Are we somehow to *infer* the possession of the irreducible property of being a dog from the possession of some other, more tangible, properties? If so, how again? What would be the nature of the inference, or the source of its validation?

Matters are exacerbated when we recall the 'shmog' example, and the fact that Tanya fails to believe that Gustav is a shmog, even though shmogs and dogs comprise a single biological species. For if one were to claim that 'dog' expressed a primitive and irreducible property, then one would be further constrained to hold that 'shmog' expressed a *different* primitive and irreducible property. Are there, then, in Plato's heaven infinitely many primitive and irreducible properties just like doghood but for their being uninstantiated?

Surely we must not suppose that Gustav, in addition to having a certain appearance, demeanour, morphology, ancestry, genetic structure, and so on, also has, over and above all these properties, the entirely distinct, primitive and irreducible property of being a dog.[10]

---

[10] Here it must be kept in mind that what is at issue is the existence of a *language-independent* property of being a dog, something that could be the meaning of 'dog'. Thus the irreducibility of the *predicate* '*x* is a dog' would not of itself prove that there was an irreducible language-independent *property* of being a dog, but might itself be a premiss in an argument to show that there was no such property. See below, section 7.

In this way I am led to conclude that the classical theory of Tanya's belief is false: the complete content of her belief, when she believes that Gustav is a dog, is not ⟨Gustav, the property of being a dog⟩. For the best candidate for being the property of being a dog (if there really is such a property) is the property of belonging to *Canis familiaris*, the biological natural kind to which all and only dogs belong (if there really is such a natural kind); but ⟨ ⟨Gustav, *Canis familiaris*⟩, the kind-membership relation⟩ cannot, we have seen, be the complete content of Tanya's belief.

To say that (3) is not the content of Tanya's belief is by no means to say that the propositionalist cannot account for it, or for (2), the sentence which ascribes it. But what moves has this theorist now at his disposal? To answer this we must (*a*) take stock of what is left to the propositionalist and (*b*) see his plight on analogy with the problem he faces as regards modes of presentation and the complete contents of *de re* beliefs about material particulars. This deserves its own section.

4. BELIEFS ABOUT NATURAL KINDS

Assume that belief contents are propositions. Then there is some proposition that is the content of the belief Tanya expressed when she uttered (1), and this proposition may or may not be the referent of 'that Gustav is a dog' as it occurs in (2). At all events, we know that, even given our ongoing simplifying assumption about the role of 'Gustav', the proposition (3), ⟨Gustav, doghood⟩, is not the content of Tanya's belief. At the same time we are still justified— given the assumption that the propositional theory of belief is true!—in maintaining, first, that 'is a dog' in (2) occurs there as *at least* referring to doghood, and, second, that the best candidate for doghood (given that there is such a property) is belonging to the natural kind *Canis familiaris*. We have just finished the case for the second position, but it may be worth rehearsing the case for the first. Here the point is simply this: on a propositionalist rendering of (2), 'Tanya believes that Gustav is a dog', each semantically relevant constituent of the content sentence 'Gustav is a dog' is referential; 'is a dog' is clearly a semantically relevant constituent; and its reference must at least include doghood, since (2) is true in any given possible world only if Tanya has in that world a belief that is true only if Gustav has the property of being a dog (although, as we shall later observe, this does not entail that the proposition that is the content of Tanya's belief either contains doghood or entails that Gustav is a dog). What all this suggests is, so to say, that (2) ascribes to Tanya a belief that is *de re* with respect to *Canis familiaris*, and that the proposition which is the complete content of her belief contains a *mode of presentation* of that species, whether or not it also includes the species. The proper amplification of these dense words requires us now to change the subject a little.

Suppose that Ralph says, quite sincerely,

(*a*) She's clever,

'she' there referring to Emily. The propositionalist, by definition, holds that there is some proposition *p* that is the complete content of the belief Ralph expressed in uttering (*a*); *p* must be such that, in this, the actual, world it is true just in case Emily is clever, but it will presently be evident that that need not be its truth condition in all possible worlds. In fact it is clear that the complete content of Ralph's belief cannot be the singular proposition

(*b*) ⟨Emily, cleverness⟩,

which proposition is true in any given possible world just in case Emily is clever in that world. For, as regards the complete content of the belief expressed by Ralph in uttering (*a*), it is clear that he does not both believe and disbelieve it: *nothing* will induce Ralph sincerely to utter 'She is not clever' in the very circumstances in which he utters (*a*). And yet, Ralph might encounter Emily in a new circumstance, and, failing to recognize her as the subject of his earlier judgement, now pronounce,

(*c*) She (unlike the other one) is not clever.

If the content of the belief Ralph expressed in uttering (*c*) were ⟨Emily, non-cleverness⟩, then we should, contrary to hypothesis, have to say that Ralph both believed and disbelieved that proposition which was the complete content of the belief he expressed in uttering (*a*). Of course, to anticipate the point we are coming to, the propositionalist wants here to borrow a move from Frege and say that there are distinct modes of presentation, *m* and *m'*, such that Ralph believes Emily to be clever under *m* but believes her not to be clever under m', m and m' being constituents of the propositions providing the contents of the beliefs expressed in the two utterances. Thus Ralph, in his utterance of (c), is not expressing disbelief in that proposition in which he expressed belief by his utterance of (a), but rather disbelief in a quite distinct proposition, one which contains m', a distinct mode of presentation of Emily from m, the one contained in the content of the belief expressed in (a).[11]

Imagine now a slightly changed scenario, in which, in place of (a) and (c), we have utterances, in different circumstances, of

(a') I believe that she's clever

and

(c') I believe that she's not clever,

both occurrences of 'she' referring, unbeknown to Ralph, to one and the same person, Emily. And let us further suppose that both utterances are true, and that 'believes' in (a') and (c') expresses the dyadic belief relation between an agent and a proposition, that relation B such that, if B (x, p), then p is the complete content of x's belief that p.[12] Then, needless to say, (a') and (c') can*not* be correctly represented respectively as

B (Ralph, ⟨Emily, cleverness⟩)

and

B (Ralph, ⟨Emily, non-cleverness⟩).

Yet 'she' in both (a') and (c') *does* refer to Emily. How, then, is the propositionalist to account for the logical forms of these utterances?

Well, he might appeal to 'modes of presentation' and represent (a') as

(d) (Em) (m is a mode of presentation of Emily & B (Ralph, ⟨m, cleverness⟩)).

This does not identify for us the proposition providing the complete

---

[11] Frege (1960); Schiffer (1977, 1978, 1981).

[12] 'Believes' in (a') and (c') *need* not be this dyadic relation. It could, for example, be construed as a triadic relation, $^rB (x, ⟨y_1, \ldots, y_n⟩, F^n)$, which relates a believer to an n-ary sequence of items and an n-ary relation; then the propositionalist would reduce ^rB to B. In the end, these are, for the propositionalist, little more than notational matters, the assumption of the text a useful expedient, as well as the most plausible position for the propositionalist to take. See Schiffer (1978, 1981).

content of the belief Ralph expressed when he uttered (a); it merely tells us that that proposition contains *some* mode of presentation of Emily. The proposition $\langle m, \text{cleverness} \rangle$ is true in a possible world w just in case whatever m is a mode of presentation of in w is clever in w.[13] Since m is in fact a mode of presentation of Emily, we know that $\langle m, \text{cleverness} \rangle$ is true in the actual world if and only if Emily is clever; perhaps—a point to be touched on later (but not one of much importance to present issues)—in other possible worlds m is not a mode of presentation of Emily, and in those worlds the truth of $\langle m, \text{cleverness} \rangle$ will be independent of the existence of Emily in them.

Suppose, now, that m^* is the mode of presentation that makes (d) true; that is to say, that $\langle m^*, \text{cleverness} \rangle$ is the complete content of the belief Ralph expressed in uttering (a). Then we know that Ralph does not also believe $\langle m^*, \text{non-cleverness} \rangle$. But that of course will not preclude our theorist from representing (c') as

(*e*) (Em) (m is a mode of presentation of Emily & B (Ralph, $\langle m, \text{non-cleverness} \rangle$)),

for the mode of presentation that makes (e) true will be a different mode of presentation of Emily than the one that makes (d) true.[14]

What are these 'modes of presentation'? That is, what sort of

---

[13] Our notation for representing propositions, admitting both $\langle \text{Emily, cleverness} \rangle$ and $\langle m, \text{cleverness} \rangle$, would be something less than perspicuous if it mattered.

[14] The theorist of modes of presentation *can* represent (a') as (d) (and (c') as (e), though they can be ignored for the present), but need not. There are two possible ways in which he might wish to depart from this way of representing (a'). First, he might want to construe (a') as containing an implicit indexical requiring reference to a mode of presentation or type of mode of presentation in order to accommodate a certain context-relativity endemic to *de re* ascriptions (see Schiffer (1977, 1978)). Second, while a theorist might agree that the mere singular proposition $\langle \text{Emily, cleverness} \rangle$ could not be the complete content of Ralph's belief, he might also feel that there could be no specification of that content that did not include a reference to Emily, and that, therefore, she, too, along with the mode of presentation, must be a constituent of whatever proposition was the content. For this theorist, (a') should be represented as

(Em) (m is a mode of presentation of Emily & B (Ralph, $\langle \langle m, \text{Emily} \rangle$, cleverness $\rangle$)),

$\langle \langle m, \text{Emily} \rangle, \text{cleverness} \rangle$ being a proposition that is true in a possible world w just in case Emily is clever in w. Here m makes no contribution to the proposition's truth value, its job being to determine a functional role for the belief which secures its satisfaction of Frege's Constraint (see Schiffer (1978) and below).

Although I shall later touch on the second one again, both of these complexities may be safely ignored in the present discussion.

thing constitutes the range of values of the objectual variable '*m*'? 'Mode of presentation' is a theoretical term, defined by its role in the theory of belief that has recourse to it. There may not be any modes of presentation—there may not be things that have the roles determined by 'mode of presentation' in the theory that speaks of modes of presentation—and if there are modes of presentation, we certainly do not yet know what they are; we do not, that is, know what things, if any, play the roles that must be played if there are to be modes of presentation. For the propositionalist, a mode of presentation is whatever language-independent entity completes the content of a *de re* belief when all that one is given initially is that a certain thing is believed by so and so to be such and such, and, as such, it must satisfy certain constraints, paramount among them being one that I have elsewhere called 'Frege's Constraint', a constraint which any candidate must satisfy if it is to qualify as a mode of presentation, namely:

Necessarily, if *m* is a mode of presentation under which a minimally rational person *x* believes a thing *y* to be *F*, then it is not the case that *x* also believes *y* not to be *F* under *m*. In other words, if *x* believes *y* to be *F* and also believes *y* not to be *F*, then there are distinct modes of presentation *m* and *m'* such that *x* believes *y* to be *F* under *m* and disbelieves *y* to be *F* under *m'*.[15]

Since singular propositions such as ⟨Emily, cleverness⟩ cannot be complete contents, it is crucial to the propositional theory of propositional attitudes that there be modes of presentation satisfying Frege's Constraint. But it is a substantial question as to whether there are any. Actually, I am nowadays very doubtful that there are things suitable to the propositionalist that can serve as modes of presentation to enter into the complete contents of our *de re* beliefs about material particulars.[16] But that is not our present concern,

---

[15] Schiffer (1978), p. 180.

[16] In Schiffer (1977, 1978) I plumped for a version of the description theory of *de re* thought, but I now think that that view requires people to have beliefs of a complexity and degree of sophistication that it is doubtful they can have. Thus, six-year-old Johnny has a visual memory of someone he glimpsed, and says, referring to that person, 'She was a nice lady'. Surely, the child believes of the woman he saw that she was nice, but it seems to me psychologically implausible to suppose that the complete content of his belief is that there is a woman who is uniquely such that his visual image is a memory image of her, and who is also nice. A number of writers have suggested that 'percept-tokens' be taken to be the modes of presentation entering into perceptual, *de re* beliefs (see, e.g., Bach (1982), Davies (unpublished),

which is to challenge the propositionalist to provide a plausible account of beliefs involving natural-kind concepts like *dog*. Still, I should like briefly to rehearse one famous possible answer to the question of what modes of presentation for material particulars might be; this not for its own sake, but for its relevance to the forthcoming question of what might, for the propositionalist, be the mode of presentation of *Canis familiaris* that enters into the complete content of Tanya's belief that Gustav is a dog.

The famous view I allude to is the one associated with Frege and Russell, that modes of presentation are *individual concepts*, typically 'indexicalized' by irreducible occurrences in their specifications of 'I' and 'now'. If P is any property, then it determines the individual concept, **the P**, which is the property of having P uniquely; so, a thing x instantiates **the P** provided that x has P and nothing else does. The general property P might contain, so to speak, oneself and the present moment; it might be the property of being now related to oneself in way R, whence the individual concept it determined would be that expressed by the definite description 'the thing that is R to me now'. On this Frege–Russell, description-theoretic reduction of *de re* thought, (d), the canonical representation of (a'), gives way to

(f) (EP) (Emily instantiates **the P** and B (Ralph, $\langle$**the P**, cleverness$\rangle$)).

Here the *general* proposition

(g) $\langle$**the P**, cleverness$\rangle$

contains not the P, which is Emily, but the uniqueness property, **the P**, which she instantiates; and the proposition is true in a possible world w iff whatever instantiates **the P in** w is clever in w. Typically, individual concepts—**the president of France in 1984**, **the woman with whom I am now speaking**, **the husband of Nancy**—are contingent properties of the things which instantiate them. Thus, not only does (g) not contain Emily, but, if P is a contingent property of hers, as it almost certainly would be, then it does not even entail that Emily is

Loar (1981), and Peacocke (1981, 1983). However, it seems clear that this view is credible only if there is some function f such that

a percept-token n is a mode of presentation of x iff $f(n) = x$,

and I am very doubtful that anyone can succeed in saying what that function is (here I am indebted to Keith Quillen).

clever (since (g) will be true in possible worlds in which Emily is not clever but the P in that world is). At the same time, if we assume that 'Emily' and 'Ralph' in (f) are rigid designators, then (f) (and thus (a')) will be true in a possible world w only if Ralph believes in w a proposition that is true in w just in case Emily is clever in w.

For the propositionalist whom we have brought to this point there is a striking parallel between (2), 'Tanya believes that Gustav is a dog', and (a'), 'I believe that she's clever'. For, as regards (2), the theorist wants to say that, whereas 'is a dog' in (2) refers to doghood, the singular proposition ⟨Gustav, doghood⟩ is not the complete content of Tanya's belief. And, as regards (a'), the theorist wants to say that, whereas 'she' in (a') refers to Emily, ⟨Emily, cleverness⟩ is not the complete content of Ralph's belief. The propositionalist is now motivated to find a mode of presentation for doghood to enter into the proposition that is the complete content of Tanya's belief. But the property of being a dog has, for the propositionalist, in the meantime transpired to be the property of belonging to *Canis familiaris*, the natural kind to which, in fact, all and only dogs belong. The theorist's recourse to modes of presentation will thus be manifested, roughly speaking, in his representation of (2) as

(A) (Em) (m is a mode of presentation of *Canis familiaris* & B (Tanya, ⟨ ⟨Gustav, m⟩, the kind-membership relation⟩)).

This is speaking roughly because the theorist, mindful of maintaining a certain position about the possible-worlds truth conditions of natural-kind beliefs, might prefer

(B) (Em) (m is a mode of presentation of *Canis familiaris* & B (Tanya, ⟨ ⟨Gustav, ⟨m, *Canis familiaris*⟩ ⟩, the kind-membership relation⟩))

to (A), as the proposition believed in (B) contains the species along with the mode of presentation of it.[17] Fortunately, however, the

[17] See n. 14. Even though for the present discussion the option introduced by (B) can safely be ignored, however unproblematic it might be, I do think that this way of representing (2) faces difficulties over and above those facing (A). For, first, the representation of (2) as (B) is coherent only if m need not *uniquely* determine that which it is a mode of presentation of—in this case, *Canis familiaris* (for if m did uniquely determine *Canis familiaris*, then the occurrence of the species in the

sort of subtleties introduced by (B) can safely be ignored, and the pretence safely maintained that (A) is the only relevant option, for we shall be able to argue against candidate modes of presention for the species of dogs quite independently of the question of whether they would best be housed in a format of the type of (A) or of the type of (B).

So, let us suppose that the propositionalist, in recognizing the failure of the classical theory of Tanya's belief, recognizes (subject to the foregoing simplification) that the representation of (2) as (A) is his last remaining hope. What, then, might the mode of presentation of the species of dogs be that is supposed to be a constituent of that proposition which is the complete content of Tanya's belief that Gustav is a dog?

I can think of only two possible proposals.

The first would be a description-theoretic account of Tanya's concept *dog*, a view which holds that in believing that Gustav is a dog, she believes of the species, under some individual concept, that Gustav belongs to it. Curiously, a description-theoretic approach to beliefs about natural kinds is the sort of positive account suggested by the informal glosses of Kripke and Putnam, official pronouncements against the decried description theory notwithstanding.

The second proposal is that the mode of presentation entering into Tanya's belief is the *stereotype* of dogs, roughly, the doggy *Gestalt*, or, to give it a topically 'scientific' gloss, a *prototype* of dogs.[18]

These proposals will soon be given their due; first, in the next section, I want, independently of considering possible modes of presentation for the species of dogs, to give some reasons why this mode-of-presentation approach is, in the case of Tanya's belief, misguided.

5. REASONS FOR BEING DOUBTFUL THAT THE BELIEF THAT. . . DOG. . . IS A BELIEF ABOUT THE SPECIES OF DOGS UNDER A MODE OF PRESENTATION

The propositionalist, having despaired of the classical solution, now

---

proposition would be unmotivated); but, second, I do not see how a mode of presentation could satisfy Frege's Constraint if it did not uniquely determine that which it was a mode of presentation of.

[18] See, e.g., the discussion and references in Smith and Medin (1981).

suggests that the complete content of Tanya's belief (relative to ongoing simplifying assumptions) is

$$\langle \langle Gustav, m \rangle, \text{the kind-membership relation} \rangle,$$

where m is a mode of presentation of the species of dogs.

I doubt, for the following two reasons, that this mode-of-presentation solution can be correct.

(1) If the propositionalist who has recourse to modes of presentation is to provide us with an adequate account of the proposition we seek, then that account must cohere with the following three facts.

(*a*) There cannot be a *unique* proposition that must be the content of Tanya's belief, because there cannot be a *unique* mode of presentation under which each person who believes that something is a dog has his or her belief about the species of dogs. If a belief such as Tanya's is about the species of dogs under a mode of presentation, then it must be allowed that different modes of presentation, different ways of thinking about doghood, could sustain a belief that . . . dog . . . I take this to be fairly obvious in view of the fact that Irish wolfhounds, German shepherds, poodles, chihuahuas, and dachshunds are all dogs, while timber-wolves, coyotes, and jackals are not, and in view of the fact that it is perfectly possible that each of the following people might have, or have had, the belief that Gustav was a dog: Tanya, who is one of us; Helen Keller; a man who, though he has seen a few dogs, is as ignorant about them as Putnam is about elms and birches; a person who has never encountered a dog, but has read about them; a child who has no biological sophistication whatever, and would obdurately persist in calling a Twin-Earth, dog-like non-dog a dog even after having been apprised of the creature's genetic dissimilarity to our dogs.

(*b*) The predicate 'believes that something is a dog', unlike, say, the predicate 'believes that he is in love with her' is a semantically complete, univocal predicate which any given person at any given time either satisfies or fails to satisfy; that is, it is not ambiguous, and seems not to contain hidden indexical parameters.

(*c*) It is not sufficient for believing that Gustav is a dog that, for some mode of presentation m, one believes of the species dog, under m, that Gustav belongs to it. This is evident from the fact that one can believe that Gustav is of such and such a biochemically described genotype without believing that he is a dog, even though the genotype is the one constitutive of the species.

If the theorist of modes of presentation is to make his position cohere with (*a*) to (*c*), then he must claim that there is a certain class *C* of modes of presentation such that (2) is logically equivalent to

(E*m*) (*m* is a mode of presentation of *Canis familiaris* & B (Tanya, ⟨ ⟨Gustav, *m*⟩, the kind-membership relation⟩) & *m* belongs to *C*).

But, quite frankly, *I doubt that anyone has the slightest idea of how C is to be specified*. This is not, of course, to say that there might not be plausible candidates for membership in *C*, and in fact two sorts of candidates (later to be considered on their own merits) have already been mentioned; but that still does not leave us with any suggestion as to how *C* is to be specified.

(2) There is a striking disanalogy between the present mode-of-presentation account of beliefs whose contents are specifiable using 'dog' and the mode-of-presentation account of those cases for which modes of presentation were first introduced and where recourse to them must be legitimate if the propositional theory of belief is true. An instance of that paradigmatic application is (*a'*), 'I believe that she's clever', in section 3, where we wanted to say that Ralph's belief about Emily was of her under some mode of presentation *precisely because* an utterance of (*c'*), 'I believe that she is not clever', reference again to Emily, might *also* be true. Let us call this 'the belief/disbelief phenomenon'; it occurs when ostensibly contradictory beliefs are correctly ascribed to a person without any imputation of irrationality. What is striking about a sentence such as

(D) Tanya believes that dogs bark

is that

(~D) Tanya believes that dogs do not bark

cannot, consistently with Tanya's being rational, concurrently be true. Tanya's belief seems not to exhibit the belief/disbelief phenomenon.[19] This gives us the wherewithal to show that the mode-of-presentation account of Tanya's belief is false. For:

(1) The view in question has it that (D) is equivalent to
   (i) (E*m*) (*m* is a mode of presentation of *Canis familiaris* & . . . & B (Tanya, . . . *m* . . .))).

[19] Cf. Schiffer (1978), p. 178.

(2) So, by parity of reasoning, the view also holds that (~D) is equivalent to
   (*ii*) (E*m'*) (. . . & B (Tanya, *not* . . . *m'* . . .)).

(3) Now (*i*) is certainly consistent with (*ii*). (That is to say, if Tanya believes the species of dogs to be F under one mode of presentation, *m*, then she can certainly also believe the species *not* to be F under a distinct mode of presentation, *m'*.)

(4) Therefore, (D) and (~D) can concurrently be true consistently with Tanya's being rational, if the mode-of-presentation view is correct.

(5) But, we know, (D) and (~D) cannot, consistently with Tanya's being rational, concurrently be true.

(6) Therefore, the view in question is false.[20]

At the close of the last section we noticed that there were two candidate accounts for what the mode of presentation of doghood might be in a paradigm normal case such as Tanya's—namely, individual concepts of the species of dogs and the doggy 'stereotype'; they are, in fact, the only two candidates that *I* can think of. We may consolidate our case against the mode-of-presentation account of Tanya's belief by discrediting each of those candidates. Let us begin with the description-theoretic treatment of Tanya's belief.

6. INDIVIDUAL CONCEPTS AS MODES OF PRESENTATION OF DOGHOOD

In the last section I offered two very general reasons for doubting that there is any correct mode-of-presentation treatment of the contents of beliefs ascribable with 'dog', *a fortiori* of Tanya's belief that Gustav is a dog. At the same time, there are two proposals as to what the mode of presentation might be, at least in a paradigm case

---

[20] This argument can also be run on 'Tanya believes that Gustav is a dog', but then it would be important to keep in mind our stipulation about 'Gustav': it is irrelevant that Gustav can be believed and disbelieved by Tanya to be a dog, for the argument concerns the belief/disbelief phenomenon with respect to 'dog'. Suppose that 'Gustav' introduced the individual concept **the G** into the complete content of Tanya's belief; then the point would be that 'Tanya believes that the G is a dog' and 'Tanya believes that the G is *not* a dog' could not, consistently with her being rational, concurrently be true.

such as Tanya's, and we cannot afford to dismiss the general theory without considering the specific forms it might take.

The description-theoretic proposal, in short (and relative to our simplifying assumption about Gustav), is this. The correct representation of (2), 'Tanya believes that Gustav is a dog', is

> (P) (E*P*) (*Canis familiaris* instantiates **the *P*** & B (Tanya,
> ⟨ ⟨Gustav, ***the P***⟩, the kind-membership relation⟩)).

(This does not *overthrow* (A) as the correct representation of (2), but purports to show what (A) comes to once it is revealed that modes of presentation are individual concepts.)

In other words, there is some individual concept ***the P*** such that the species of dogs, *Canis familiaris*, instantiates ***the P*** and Tanya believes *that Gustav belongs to the P*. This proposition, *that Gustav belongs to the P*, is the complete content of Tanya's belief; it is true in a possible world *w* iff Gustav belongs in *w* to whatever in *w* instantiates ***the P***; as it happens, in this world ***the P*** is instantiated by *Canis familiaris*, the natural kind to which all of our dogs (and nothing else) belong, and therefore (2) is true. In believing that Gustav is a dog, Tanya believes of the species *Canis familiaris*, under the mode of presentation ***the P***, that Gustav belongs to it.[21]

Now what might the proponent of this solution have in mind as the individual concept under which Tanya has her belief about the species of dogs? It will not do to say that it is the individual concept expressed by 'the kind to which those creatures belong', where 'those creatures' refers to some paradigmatic dogs; for there will, of course, be several kinds to which those creatures belong—animal, mammal, canine, dog, cocker spaniel, male, etc. A more plausible suggestion is that it is the individual concept expressed by 'the species of those things', 'those things' understood as before, the idea being that the content of Tanya's belief is that Gustav belongs to the species of such and such creatures. But this, as it stands, will not do either: even supposing the role of 'those creatures' to be fixed and unproblematic, the term 'species' in ordinary language is

---

[21] As stated, (P) is not strictly the hypothesis we need, as it fails to state a sufficient condition for the truth of (2). To get a sufficient condition we should have to add 'and ***the P*** belongs to *C*', where *C* is the class of individual concepts that allows the use of 'dog' in ascriptions of content (if (*a*) one believes that Lulu belongs to the same species as the species of George's pet, and (*b*) George's pet is a dog, it does not follow that (*c*) one believes that Lulu is a dog). But we may help the description theorist by ignoring this qualification in the ensuing discussion.

vague and ambiguous, and, consequently, the phrase 'the species of those things' determines no individual concept independently of some specified reading of 'species'. It would seem that the intended reading of 'species' must be 'biological species', if we can momentarily pretend that that expression succeeds in introducing a definite property.[22] However, it is most implausible to suppose that Tanya believes that Gustav belongs to the biological species of such and such creatures when she believes that Gustav is a dog. One reason, of course, is that we must not suppose her to be in any way sophisticated about biology; but an even better reason emerges thus.

Consider

(*i*) Tanya believes that Henry is a rabbit,

which belief happens to be true: Henry is a rabbit. If it is plausible to construe (2) in the way under consideration, then, by parity of reasoning, the complete content of Tanya's belief about Henry should be given by

(*ii*) Tanya believes that Henry belongs to the biological species of those creatures,

the reference here being to a fairly comprehensive sample of paradigm rabbits. But this cannot be right, as (*i*) ascribes to Tanya a true belief, whereas (*ii*) ascribes to her a false belief: rabbits do not constitute a single biological species, but rather an assortment of animals of the biological family *Leporidae* for which there is no better taxonomic term than 'rabbit'.

Perhaps, more promisingly, what Tanya really believes about Gustav is that he shares the internal properties, whatever they turn out to be, which causally account for such and such observable characteristics commonly found among so and so creatures, the latter reference again being to a wide assortment of paradigm dogs. There are, however, two problems with this suggestion. First, it is absurd to suppose that this could represent the belief of a nine-year-old child, or even of an ordinary, but biologically unreflective, adult. Second, the suggestion presupposes, in effect, that there is a complex genetic property, a genotype, common to all and only dogs, but this, I think, is also doubtful. A German shepherd and a

[22] And it is far from clear that it does. Se Kitcher (unpublished).

timber-wolf are capable of interbreeding and of having fertile offspring; they also look very much alike, much more alike than, say, a German shepherd and a French poodle. It is a good bet that there is no genotype shared by the German shepherd, the French poodle, and all other dogs but which excludes the timber-wolf, not to mention the coyote, the dingo, and the jackal.

I dare say that the prospects are looking bleak for (P). We are assuming that there is a natural kind to which all and only dogs belong, and (P) requires us to find a property P such that, first, P is uniquely instantiated by that kind and, second, P might reasonably be thought to be a constituent of the content of an ordinary person's belief that . . . dog. . . . But I believe that the foregoing reveals the questionableness of there being any non-metalinguistic property that satisfies both these requirements. Might there, however, be a *metalinguistic* individual concept that does the description theorist's trick? The thought will already have occurred to this theorist in connection with beliefs the contents of which are specifiable with words like 'arthritis', 'felony', 'elm' and 'electron'. Now it is surely preposterous to think that *all* kind concepts are metalinguistic; yet that is what we would clearly be driven to if we were to suppose that the complete content of Tanya's belief *had* to include a metalinguistic individual concept that was instantiated by *Canis familiaris*. At any rate, here is another reason for scotching the description theorist's final, desperate effort, followed by a further reason for rejecting in this area any sort of recourse to individual concepts of natural kinds.

(*a*) Exactly *what* metalinguistic individual concept is supposed to enter into that proposition that is the complete content of Tanya's belief? Certainly not *the kind the experts call 'dog'*; at least not until we are told what experts (experts in animals? or in animal speciation? or in what?), and what semantic relation is to be introduced by the infirm verb 'call' ('denotes'? 'is true of'? and what relations do those terms introduce, anyway?). Actually, I seriously doubt that there really is any clearly specifiable metalinguistic property uniquely true of the kind *dog*; but that is not a line I wish now to pursue. Instead, I shall let this be my first objection: if one were ever to succeed in specifying clearly and precisely a metalinguistic individual concept instantiated by the kind to which all and only dogs belonged, then it would simply be obvious that no ordinary person had the semantic and technical expertise that he or she would have to have in order for that individual concept to enter into the contents of his or her beliefs about dogs.

(*b*) Let us, following Russell, say that one is *acquainted* with a property Q if Q occurs unaccompanied by a mode of presentation of it in some proposition that is the complete content of one of one's beliefs; perhaps redness and squareness are objects of acquaintance. Then the objection may be put thus. Assume that *the P* is an individual concept instantiated by the species of dogs. Then P will itself be a logically complex property concocted out of properties such as *natural kind, animal, expert, denotes, genotype*, etc. Now if doghood cannot be a constituent of a belief content, but must have in its place an individual concept which it instantiates, then that must surely be true also of at least some of the properties out of which P is concocted. Therefore, *the P* could not occur in the proposition that was the content of one's belief that so and so was a dog, for certain properties in P would no more be items of acquaintance than doghood is, and would require their own modes of presentation. Therefore, if one's belief about the species of dogs is under an individual concept, that individual concept must be composed wholly of properties with which one is acquainted. Now *what on earth* could even be a candidate for such a mode of presentation?

Several philosophers, thinking themselves well defended against the sallies from the New Theory of Reference, have remained attracted to the Frege–Russell description theory of beliefs that are *de re* with respect to material particulars other than oneself.[23] For such philosophers, a description-theoretic treatment of beliefs involving natural-kind concepts is a natural temptation; but the considerations adduced in this section show not only that that is a temptation to be resisted, but also that one cannot rest content with a description-theoretic reduction of beliefs about material particulars independently of a plausible line on the properties that are supposed to compose the individual concepts, of particulars, to which the theorist makes appeal. We are in the midst of seeing that this is no easy task.

[23] See, e.g., Loar (1976) and Schiffer (1978).

7. STEREOTYPES AS MODES OF PRESENTATION OF DOGHOOD

Here the suggestion is that, in a paradigmatic case such as Tanya's, we might take the 'concept' (insidious word!) *dog* to be an observational concept in the visual mode, and, in line with this, take the mode of presentation under which Tanya has her belief about the species to be her 'stereotype' of the species, her 'prototype' of it, something like the doggy *Gestalt*. Let D be such a stereotype for Tanya; the suggestion is then that D enters directly into the proposition that is the content of her belief that Gustav is a dog. It should be noticed that for this hypothesis to have any chance of success, it must not be required that Gustav fits D, for Tanya can believe him to be a dog even if he is an egregious mutant; nor must it be required that she believe that D is in any way *uniquely* true of dogs; for, if that were required, then we should merely have another version of the already discredited description theory. The idea must simply be that the presence of D in the content of Tanya's belief secures its satisfaction of Frege's Constraint, and somehow makes the belief, or helps to make it, about *Canis familiaris*. I have been charitable to this hypothesis in not trying to state it precisely (what, precisely, are these 'stereotypes' supposed to be, anyway?), but here are two reasons for doubting it even as stated.

(1) The proponent of this hypothesis will need an account of what makes D a mode of presentation *of the species of dogs*. He needs, in other words, a relation R such that

> D is a mode of presentation of *Canis familiaris* iff R (D, *Canis familiaris*).

R cannot, we have noticed, be an instantiation relation. Evidently, one will seek some suitable *causal* relation. But what suitable causal relation? This may not be such an easy thing to find if one keeps rabbits in mind. For suppose that Tanya has only seen pet rabbits. How can the resultant *Gestalt*, or stereotype, then succeed in being of the larger natural kind which includes hares? But that is precisely what it must do if we are to account on the proposed lines for her belief that Henry is a rabbit.

(2) No matter; it is doubtful in any event that D can satisfy Frege's Constraint, which really provides *the* motivation for the introduction of modes of presentation. It seems clear that, in

principle, D could be a mode of presentation of more than one natural kind; after all, my Twin-Earth counterpart's stereotype of the non-dogs he calls 'dogs' will be the same as mine, and there is nothing to prevent tdogs from inhabiting Earth, which could certainly lead to my dog-stereotype being of two distinct zoological species. But then I might become aware that there were two distinct species sharing my stereotype. And if this were possible, then it is difficult to see what could prevent my believing and disbelieving the species of dogs to be such and such under one and the same mode of presentation—namely, D—thus violating Frege's Constraint. For, if I can believe that dogs but not tdogs are F, then I can certainly misidentify dogs as tdogs and believe, of the species to which they (the dogs misidentified as tdogs) belong, under D, that its members are not F, when I already believe, of the species, also under D, that its members are F. If we are ever to take seriously the idea that beliefs such as Tanya's are made complete by the presence in them of doggy stereotypes, we shall certainly require an articulation and treatment of that intuition that elevates it into an hypothesis worth considering.

That concludes my argument against the propositional theory of belief, which may be summarized as follows:

> If that theory were true, then some proposition would be the content of Tanya's belief that Gustav was a dog, and that proposition would either contain doghood itself or a 'mode of presentation' of it. But if there really is a genuinely language-independent property of doghood, then doghood is the property of belonging to the biological natural kind to which all and only dogs belong (if there is such a natural kind), and once this is appreciated it is easy to show, with examples like the 'shmog' example, that doghood cannot itself be the propositional constituent we seek. Then the case against modes of presentation is overdetermined: the theory that the contents of natural-kind beliefs contain modes of presentation of the kinds can be argued against independently of specific proposals about the nature of those modes of presentation; and the two specific proposals considered (the only ones I can think of) were found to be unsatisfactory. So I conclude that there is no proposition that can plausibly be taken to be the content of a belief such as Tanya's,

and therefore that the propositional theory of propositional attitudes is false.

I also have a further reason for thinking that there is no proposition to be the content of Tanya's belief: there is one only if there really exists a non-pleonastic, genuinely language-independent property of being a dog; but there is no such property. I will not now set out the argument for denying that there is a property of being a dog, but it in no way proceeds from nominalist premises, and its gist may be conveyed thus.

(1) If there were a (non-pleonastic, language-independent) property of being a dog, it would not be irreducible: we are not to suppose that Gustav, in addition to having a certain appearance, demeanour, morphology, ancestry, genetic structure, and so on, also has, over and above all these properties, the quite distinct, primitive and irreducible property of being a dog. (2) If there were a reducible property of being a dog, there would be some property, however logically complex, specifiable in phenotypic and/or genetic and/or evolutionary, etc. terms which *was* the property of being a dog. (3) But there is no such property which is the property of being a dog; none of Gustav's properties, however complex, is such that, necessarily, a thing is a dog if and only if it has that property (part of my reason for thinking this is the point made earlier, in section 6, that there is, evidently, no gene pool common to all and only dogs).

As I said, the case against the propositional theory may be overdetermined.

8. POSTSCRIPT: COMPOSITIONAL SEMANTICS AND THE RELATIONAL THEORY OF PROPOSITIONAL ATTITUDES

Well, if propositions are not the relata of the belief relation, what are the relata? What, if not propositions, are the values of the objectual variable 'p' in the schema 'x believes p'?

Nothing else, I am inclined to answer. Propositions are at least as well suited as anything else to be the objects of belief, if beliefs have objects (and if propositions exist). But I do not think beliefs do have objects. Believing is not a relation, 'p' in the schema not an objectual variable.

The propositional theory of believing is, we have seen, a conjunction of two claims: (1) believing is a relation between believers and values of the objectual variable 'p' in the schema 'x believes p', and

(2) propositions are the values of that variable. Many philosophers reject (2), usually on ontological grounds, but I hazard that most accept (1), the relational theory of believing. And with evident reason.

First, it is held that every natural language has a correct compositional meaning theory—a compositional meaning theory for a language L being a finitely stable theory of L which specifies the meanings of all the primitive vocabulary in L, and specifies compositional mechanisms which show how those meanings determine the meanings of the infinitely many complex expressions in L. How else, it is wondered, could one explain our ability to understand indefinitely many novel sentences, or the platitude that the meaning of a sentence is a function of its syntax and the meanings of its words? Then, it is further held that every correct compositional meaning theory for a language L is also a compositional truth-theoretic semantics for L, where a meaning theory is also a truth-theoretic semantics if it somehow manages to determine a truth condition for every utterance that can have one. This thought, that a meaning theory for a language will, *inter alia*, also be a compositional truth-theoretic semantics, voices the sentiment of the many for whom 'semantics with no treatment of truth conditions is not semantics'.[24] And at this point the motivation behind the relational theory of believing is transparent: the construing of 'believes' as a relational predicate is arguably the only feasible construing of it *relative to the assumption that natural languages have compositional truth-theoretic semantics*. For, if σ is any well-formed indicative sentence of English, then $\ulcorner$believes that $\sigma\urcorner$ is a well-formed predicate phrase. Since there are infinitely many such predicate phrases, no compositional truth-theoretic semantics, being finitely stable, can treat them as semantically primitive. A compositional truth-theoretic semantics must therefore treat 'believes' as semantically primitive; and it is arguable that the only tenable way this can be done is to treat 'believes' as a relational predicate, i.e., as a predicate with argument places for singular terms.

I agree that the relational theory of believing is true, if natural languages have compositional truth-theoretic semantics. But I think that natural languages do not have either compositional

---

[24] Lewis (1972), p. 169.

meaning theories or compositional truth-theoretic semantics. This, to be sure, raises the question of how, on that negative assumption, one is to explain language understanding, the ability of a person to go from the auditory perception of the utterance of a sentence to the knowledge of what propositional speech acts, with what truth conditions, were performed in that utterance. But these are topics for further discussion.[25, 26]

BIBLIOGRAPHY

Adams, R. M. (1974) 'Theories of Actuality', *Nous*, 5, pp. 211–31.
Bach, K. (1982) 'De Re Belief and Methodological Solipsism', in A. Woodfield (ed.), *Thought and Object* (Oxford UP).
Barwise, J. and Perry, J. (1983) *Situations and Attitudes* (MIT Press).
Bealer, G. (1982) *Quality and Concept* (Oxford UP).
Burge, T. (1978) 'Belief and Synonymy', *Journal of Philosophy*, 75, pp. 249–55.
Davies, M. (unpublished) 'Individuation and the Semantics of Demonstratives'.
Frege, G. (1960) 'On Sense and Reference', in P. Geach and M. Black (edd.), *Translations from the Philosophical Writings of Gottlob Frege* (Oxford).
—— (1967) 'The Thought: A Logical Inquiry', in P. F. Strawson (ed.), *Philosophical Logic* (Oxford UP).
Kitcher, P. (unpublished) 'Species'.
Kripke, S. A. (1980) *Naming and Necessity* (Harvard UP).
Lewis, D. K. (1972) 'General Semantics', in D. Davidson and G. Harman (edd.), *Semantics of Natural Language* (Dordrecht).
Loar, B. (1976) 'The Semantics of Singular Terms', *Philosophical Studies*, 30, pp. 353–77.
—— (1981) *Mind and Meaning* (Cambridge UP).
Peacocke, C. (1981) 'Demonstrative Thought', *Synthese*, 49.
—— (1983) *Sense and Content* (Oxford UP).
Plantinga, A. (1974) *The Nature of Necessity* (Oxford UP).
Putnam, H. (1975) 'The Meaning of "Meaning"', in K. Gunderson (ed.), *Minnesota Studies in the Philosophy of Science*, Vol. 7 (University of Minn. Press), reprinted in Putnam, *Philosophical Papers*, Vol. 2 (Cambridge UP, 1975).

[25] I discuss these matters further in Schiffer (1985, forthcoming).
[26] The comments of Brian Loar, Keith Quillen, and Richard Warner were extremely helpful to me in writing this article, as was discussion with Stewart Cohen, Jody Kraus, Keith Lehrer, and John Pollock.

Russell, B. (1959) 'Knowledge by Acquaintance and Knowledge by Description' in Robert C. Marsh (ed.) *Mysticism and Logic* (London).

Salmon, N. (1981) *Reference and Essence* (Princeton UP).

Schiffer, S. (1977) 'Naming and Knowing' in P. French, T. Uehling, and H. Wettstein (edd.), *Midwest Studies in Philosophy*, Vol. 2 (University of Minn. Press), pp. 28–41.

—— (1978) 'The Basis of Reference', *Erkenntnis*, 13, pp. 171–206.

—— (1981) 'Indexicals and the Theory of Reference', *Synthese*, 49, pp. 43–100.

—— (1985) 'Compositional Semantics and Language Understanding', in R. Grandy and R. Warner (edd.), *Philosophical Grounds of Rationality: Intentions, Categories, Ends* (Oxford UP).

—— (forthcoming) *Remnants of Meaning* (MIT Press).

Smith, E., and Medin, D. (1981) *Concepts and Categories* (Harvard UP).

Wittgenstein, L. (1958) *Philosophical Investigations* (Oxford).

CHAPTER 6

ARE BELIEF PREDICATES
SYSTEMATICALLY AMBIGUOUS?*

STEPHEN P. STICH

By 'belief predicates' I shall mean predicates like

believes that Socrates is wise,
believes that the killer is insane,
believes that someone has eaten the porridge,

and, more generally, any predicate consisting of 'believes that' (or
grammatical variants) followed by a grammatically acceptable content sentence. There is a venerable tradition which holds that these
predicates are systematically ambiguous, that they typically admit
of two or more quite distinct analyses. Though this tradition has
roots deep in the history of philosophy, modern discussion of the
topic was spurred by Quine's seminal paper (1956). Since the
publication of Quine's paper, many philosophers have offered
analyses of the various senses of belief predicates. Despite major
differences on many other points, just about everyone who has
written on the topic in the last twenty-five years has shared Quine's
view that belief predicates are indeed systematically ambiguous.
Indeed, most writers seem to assume that the existence of an
ambiguity is so obvious that it needs no argument.[1] It is this all-but-
universal assumption that I propose to question in this paper. My
thesis will be that the alleged ambiguity of belief predicates is
anything but obvious, and the tentative conclusion I shall reach is
that the issue of their ambiguity is moot.

The argument of the paper divides into two parts. In the first four
sections my goal is to reconstruct the reasoning that seems to have

* © Stephen P. Stich 1986.

[1] Since a number of readers have been misled on the point, I should stress that, as
I am using the term, 'believes' and 'believes that' do not count as belief predicates,
but only as parts or components of belief predicates. The point is an important one
since there is considerable disagreement on whether 'believes' is lexically ambiguous, though it is all but universally held that belief predicates are ambiguous, as are
the belief sentences built by appending belief predicates to names or descriptions.

led Quine and others to believe there is a systematic ambiguity, and to argue that despite its prima-facie plausibility this argument does not succeed. In the remaining three sections I shall argue that the data marshalled in the Quinean argument for ambiguity are actually a mixed bag. Some of the belief predicates Quine considers are in fact ambiguous, but this ambiguity can be traced to an ambiguity in the content sentence. As for the rest, I will urge that the question of their ambiguity has no clear-cut answer.

I. THE ARGUMENT FROM ANOMALOUS INTUITIONS

Quine contends (1956) that there are two distinct senses of 'believes' and of related locutions. One of these senses, the one that Quine labels 'notional', can be thought of as expressing a two-place relation between a person and a sentence or proposition. The other sense, which Quine labels 'relational', expresses a three-place relation that may obtain among a person, an open sentence (or attribute), and an object. Other writers have used the traditional labels *de dicto* and *de re* to mark these putative senses. However, both pairs of labels have also been used to draw a very different sort of distinction—a distinction between different *kinds of beliefs*. The failure to distinguish sharply between a putative distinction of *senses* and a putative distinction of *kinds* of belief has been a source of much mischief.[2] Throughout this paper I shall reserve 'notional' and 'relational' for the putatively distinct senses of belief locutions. In the final section of the paper *de dicto* will be pressed into service as a label for a kind of belief.

To distinguish the notional and relational senses of belief locutions, Quine proposes a number of notational devices. A particularly perspicuous idea, in the spirit of Quine's proposals but with minor modifications in detail, would be to render the notional reading of

Plato believes that Socrates is wise

as

Plato believes[n] 'Socrates is wise',

and to render the relational reading as

---

[2] Devitt (1984) does a splendid job of chronicling this mischief. I have learned a great deal from Devitt's paper, though he sees ambiguities where I do not.

Plato believes[r] ('. . . is wise', Socrates).

It is no easy matter to extract an argument for the alleged ambiguity from Quine's paper. Nor do we get much help on this point in the extensive literature spawned by Quine's essay. It often appears that both Quine and his critics take the existence of an ambiguity to be too obvious to need any defence. Still, there is what might be viewed as an implicit argument for ambiguity hinted at in Quine's paper, with similar, equally fragmentary, arguments scattered throughout the literature. All of these arguments invoke what might be called the 'anomalous intuition' strategy. This strategy proceeds by constructing a scenario—a little story—and noting that against the background of this scenario certain belief predicates evoke prima facie anomalous intuitions: they strike us as being both clearly true of a certain character in the story and clearly false of that character. The ambiguity thesis is rung in to explain this anomaly. If we interpret the predicate in one way, then, in the context of the scenario that has been constructed, it is clearly true of the character; if we interpret the predicate in another way, it is clearly false of him. And the fact that the predicate admits of these two interpretations indicates that it is ambiguous.

Now it is my contention that arguments invoking the anomalous-intuition strategy do not suffice to establish ambiguity. For, I shall argue, there are semantic phenomena other than ambiguity that might engender the anomalous intuitions that serve as data for the argument. But here I am getting ahead of myself. What I propose to do in the present section is simply to reconstruct a Quine-style argument for the ambiguity of belief predicates, modifying Quine's favoured scenario a bit to bring out the requisite intuitions as clearly as possible. My critique of the argument will be set out in the three sections that follow.

Let me begin by telling a story. The central figure in the tale is Peter Rich, who struck it rich some years ago by inventing a new industrial process. He now lives in comfortable retirement on the income produced by a factory he owns, which manufactures widgets using his secret process. One day it comes to Peter's attention that a foreign manufacturer has been using the very same process. Convinced that the foreigners could not have discovered the process on their own, Peter concludes that he has been the victim of industrial espionage perpetrated by one of his employees. At this point in our tale, we might quite naturally recount Peter's doxastic state with:

(1) Peter believes that someone who works in the factory has stolen the secret process.

Intent on discovering the culprit's identity, Peter gets a job in his own factory under the assumed name of Harry Slewth. Since he is an absentee owner, none of the plant's employees recognizes him.

The foreman of the plant is a good man named David Goodman. Some time after Slewth (i.e. Rich) comes to work at the factory, Goodman too discovers that the secret process is being used by foreign competition, and he too suspects industrial espionage. Moreover, after pondering the matter for a month or two, Goodman realizes that there is an obvious suspect. He has noted the curious behaviour of the new man, Slewth, and becomes increasingly convinced that Slewth is the spy. One evening, after confiding his suspicions to his wife, Goodman decides to return to the plant in the hope of catching the culprit red-handed. Later that evening a friend inquires about Goodman's absence, and his wife reports:

(2) David believes that someone who works in the factory has stolen the secret process.

She goes on to explain that David has returned to the plant in the hope of catching him with incriminating evidence.

At this point we can begin to see why Quine thinks belief predicates are ambiguous. Both (1) and (2) invoke the same belief predicate. But on the intended reading of (2) there is a clear implication that David has a suspect; it makes sense to ask *who* David thinks has stolen the process. This is clearly not the reading intended for (1). If someone were to ask who is the object of Peter's suspicion, he would indicate that he had misunderstood the intended meaning of (1). Of course, (2) might also have been used to report David's cognitive state after learning that the secret was out but before noting Slewth's suspicious behaviour. At that time, however, (2) in the sense intended by Mrs Goodman would have been false. Thus it appears that the belief predicate in (2) can be understood in two quite different ways. During the period after he learns that the secret is out but before he comes to suspect Slewth, this belief predicate is true of David on one reading and false on the other. Much the same, of course, can be said for (1), which is true on the intended reading, but false if the predicate is understood as intended by Mrs Goodman.

Let us elaborate our little tale a bit further. On the night Goodman returns to the plant, Slewth (i.e. Rich) has used his pass-key to get into the office, and he sets about opening the office safe. Just as he gets the safe open, Goodman bursts in on him and wrestles him to the floor. Asked to explain Goodman's action, we might well say:

(3) Goodman believed that Slewth was burgling the safe.

And Goodman himself would agree with this characterization of his belief. Now let us bring our melodrama to a close. Goodman calls the police, and when they arrive Slewth explains that he is not a burglar at all but the owner of the factory. Both Goodman and the police are incredulous, so Slewth calls his old friend the mayor, who comes down to the factory and identifies him. On their return to the police station, we might well imagine one of the officers using (4) in recounting the adventures of the evening to his amused colleagues:

(4) Goodman believed that the owner of the factory was burgling the safe.

Similarly, we can imagine the mayor using (5) while regaling the city fathers with an account of the evening:

(5) Goodman believed that Peter Rich was burgling the safe.

It seems clear that both (4) and (5) can be understood as saying something true. However, it is also clear that when the police arrived, Goodman would have vigorously denied that the belief predicates in either (4) or (5) characterized his cognitive state while wrestling Slewth to the floor. Given this obviously sincere denial, there is a strong inclination to say that (4) and (5) are false, and that both (6) and (7) can be understood as saying something true:

(6) Goodman did not believe that the owner of the factory was burgling the safe.

(7) Goodman did not believe that Peter Rich was burgling the safe.

But now we are confronting a paradox, since (6) appears to be the negation of (4), and (7) appears to be the negation of (5). How is it possible for both a sentence and its negation to say something true?

To account for our prima facie paradoxical intuitions about these sentences, Quine would invoke the doctrine of ambiguity. According to this doctrine, belief predicates generally admit of both a notional and a relational reading. Rendered into the more perspicuous notation introduced earlier, the notional reading of (4) would become

(4n) Goodman believed[n] 'the owner of the factory was burgling the safe',

while the relational reading would become

(4r) Goodman believed[r] ('. . . was burgling the safe', the owner of the factory).

Similarly, the notional reading of (6) would be

(6n) Goodman did not believe[n] 'the owner of the factory was burgling the safe',

and its relational reading would be

(6r) Goodman did not believe[r] ('. . . was burgling the safe', the owner of the factory).

On the Quinean account, when we hear (4) as saying something true, we are understanding it in the sense of (4r), while when we hear it as saying something false, we are understanding it as in (4n). Similarly, when we hear (6) as true, we are interpreting it as in (6n), and when we hear (6) as false, we are interpreting it as in (6r). Thus the paradox is resolved. (5) and (7) admit of an entirely analogous treatment. A similar analysis is obviously possible for sentences like (1) and (2). The reading on which (1) is true would be rendered

(1n) Peter believes[n] 'someone who works in the factory has stolen the secret process',

while the reading on which it is false might be rendered

(1r) (Ex) Peter believes[r] ('. . . works in the factory and has stolen the secret process', x).

In the extensive literature that has followed Quine's essay, almost everyone seems willing to agree that the paradoxical intuitions invoked by sentences like (1), (2), and (4) to (7) are evidence for the existence of an ambiguity in the belief predicates they contain. There is much less agreement on how the ambiguity is to be analysed. At one point, Quine proposed that 'believes' might itself be lexically ambiguous, and that this lexical ambiguity would account for the ambiguity of belief predicates and sentences. But many writers have found this a distinctly implausible view, and have attempted to explain the ambiguity of belief predicates on the model of a syntactic ambiguity or an ambiguity of scope. Such views typically posit a single, unambiguous, underlying term which expresses the basic notion of belief. Belief predicates are held to be analysable into the chosen primitive notation in more than one way. Thus, for example, if the basic notion of belief (expressed by 'Bel') is taken to be a relation between the believer and a sentence, then the notional reading of the belief predicate

. . . believes that Plato's teacher was wise

might be analysed quite straightforwardly as

Bel (. . ., 'Plato's teacher was wise').

The relational reading would require a more elaborate treatment, perhaps along the following lines:

(Et) (t is a name or definite description & t denotes Plato's teacher & Bel (. . ., the sentence consisting of t followed by 'is wise')).

More sophisticated treatments might require further conjuncts specifying a more intimate connection between t and the believer. By contrast, there are other theorists who take the basic notion of belief to be a three-place relation on the lines of Quine's relational sense. For these theorists, the relational reading of belief predicates can be rendered straightforwardly in primitive notation; it is the notional reading which requires more elaborate analysis.[3] But, of course, theorists on both sides agree that belief predicates are ambiguous.

I will not pause to elaborate on these alternative strategies, however, since it is my suspicion that they seek to resolve a non-existent problem. For all its intuitive appeal, I do not think that the argument from anomalous intuitions suffices to establish that belief predicates are systematically ambiguous. If they are not, then the

[3] Among those who have pursued the former strategy are Hintikka (1962, 1967, 1970), Sellars (1968), Armstrong (1973), Kaplan (1968), and perhaps Sosa (1970). For a defence of the latter strategy, see Wallace (1972), whose goals are tentatively endorsed by Hornsby (1977).

proposed analyses must all be misguided, since they all seek to explain a phenomenon which isn't there. In order to see just what is wrong with the argument from anomalous intuitions, it will be necessary to take a closer look at the notion of ambiguity itself. That is the project to which I now turn.

2. LOCATING AMBIGUITY IN SEMANTIC SPACE

The term 'ambiguous', like other commonse-sense semantic locutions is, no doubt, typically acquired by the marshalling of clear-cut examples like 'bank' and 'nut' and 'Flying planes can be dangerous'. Given a few such examples, along with examples of clear-cut cases of non-ambiguity, a person previously innocent of folk-semantic terminology can go on to classify many other cases, and to do so in a way which by and large coincides with the classifications of other speakers. This widespread agreement about an open-ended class of cases would hardly be possible unless there were some feature or cluster of features of these cases that people could exploit in making their judgements. There is a long tradition in philosophy of inferring from the existence of such an open-ended, intuitively drawable distinction to the existence of a *property* which all and only the cases falling under the term in question possess. What is more, from Plato to possible-world semantics, property possession has been thought of as binary business. Every object, indeed every possible object, either has a given property or it does not; property possession is not the sort of thing that comes in degrees. For the case at hand, the property in question is *ambiguity*, which might naturally enough be explicated as the having of more than one meaning.

It is no part of my current project to encourage general scepticism about properties or about meanings. However, a fundamental lesson to be learned from Wittgenstein, and from Rosch and her followers, is that the quick inference from the existence of an open-ended, intuitively drawable distinction to the existence of a property is often unwarranted. What Wittgenstein and Rosch have taught us is that a term can be usefully used even when there is no property which determines its extension and which speakers may attend to in deciding whether or not the term applies or fails to apply.[4] In some cases ('game' may be an example), we may judge

---

[4] I have here to run together two issues which in a more detailed treatment would

whether or not a term applies by attending to a cluster of features no one of which is either necessary or sufficient. In other cases (perhaps 'furniture'), we may judge the applicability of a term by assessing its similarity to one or more prototypical examples, along one or more dimensions. And in still other cases (like 'bald'), the applicability of a term to an object may depend on the object's place along a continuum, though there is no clearly defined point along that continuum at which the term becomes applicable. There are other possibilities as well.[5] A term whose application is determined in one of these ways, in contrast with a term whose application is determined by the presence or absence of a property, will typically not have an extension with sharp boundaries. Sometimes this will be obvious enough (as with 'bald'). But it may also happen that the difficult intermediate cases are sufficiently rare or neglected to encourage the view that the term in question applies or fails to apply in virtue of the presence or absence of a property.

What does all of this have to do with ambiguity? The answer, as you may have already have guessed, is that on my view there is no *property* of ambiguity. 'Ambiguous' is not one of those words that cleave the contents of all possible worlds into two neat classes. As I see it, 'ambiguous' is a term we apply comfortably to examples which stand close to prototypical values on a number of distinct dimensions. When we consider cases which stand further from the prototypical values on one or more of these dimensions, it becomes increasingly unclear whether to count them as ambiguous or not. Moreover, this uncertainty is not merely a matter of ignorance; it is not a matter of our just not *knowing* whether these cases are ambiguous. Rather, there simply is no fact to the matter—just as there is no fact which will settle whether a man who has lost a good deal of his hair, but far from all of it, is bald, or whether wall-to-wall carpeting is an item of furniture. All of this, of course, is compatible with there being lots of clear cases of ambiguity and of non-ambiguity, much as there are lots of clear cases of bald people and of hirsute people, and lots of things which, like the couch and easy chair in my office, clearly count as items of furniture.

---

have to be pulled apart. It is one thing for there to be a property which determines the extension of a term and quite another for speakers to attend to that property in deciding whether or not a term applies. For an excellent discussion of the distinction and its importance, see Rey (forthcoming). I think we can safely ignore the distinction for present purposes, however.

[5] See Smith and Medin (1981).

If this picture of the semantics of folk-semantic terms is on the right track, it ought to be possible to chart our intuitive semantic judgments by describing the various dimensions along which cases can vary, and then locating intuitive semantic notions in the multi-dimensional space defined by these dimensions. The idea is not that we will be able to characterize some sharp-edged n-dimensional region which determines the extension of a given semantic term. Rather, intuitive semantic notions will be associated with one (or perhaps several) points in our n-dimensional space. Expressions whose location in semantic space is close to one of these prototypical points will count as clear instances of the semantic notion in question, while expressions located further from any prototypical point will strike us as harder to classify. Obviously, a full characterization of the conceptual space of intuitive semantics would be a major undertaking, and I will make no attempt to provide such a characterization here. What I want to do instead is to develop a rough and ready characterization of some of the features that distinguish prototypical examples of ambiguous predicates. With this account in hand, we will be in a better position to assess the merits of the argument from anomalous intuitions and to decide whether belief predicates are in fact systematically ambiguous.

What is it that determines our intuitions when we judge that a predicate is clearly ambiguous? One feature that seems central is that speakers must view the overall extension of the predicate, the class of things of which it is true, as divided into two (or more) reasonably distinct categories. If '(is an) N' is an ambiguous predicate then, intuitively, there must be 'different kinds' of Ns. Thus, for example, there are different kinds of banks (those that contain money and those that contain rivers) and different kinds of nuts (those that are used as food and those that are used with bolts). In saying that the categories must be reasonably distinct, I mean that there must be some relatively clear cases of items which fall into one category but not into the other. It need not be the case, however, that there are members of each category which are not members of the other, since it may happen that one category is a proper subset of the other. 'Corn' would appear to be an example of this latter possibility, since on one reading it is true of all edible grains, while on another it is true of only one type, viz., maize. Many technical terms, in science, in the law, and elsewhere, have as their extension either a superset or a subset of the extension of the associated common-sense term. Thus, as it is used in chemistry, 'salt' has a much broader extension than it does in colloquial speech, while 'slander' in the legal sense has a more restricted extension than it does colloquially.

Though the existence of distinct categories in the extension is characteristic of predicates which intuition takes to be clearly ambiguous, this is plainly not a sufficient condition for ambiguity. There are two notably different kinds of things to be found in the extension of '(is a) parent', and many different kinds to be found in the extension of '(is an) animal'. But the existence of these kinds does not render those predicates ambiguous. What more is needed?

In trying to answer this question, I think it is useful to reflect on the following puzzle. In many languages there is a word meaning 'elder brother' and a quite different word meaning 'younger brother'. (In Mongolian the two words are *aqa* and *degu*; in Chinese they are *xiong* and *di*.) Let us suppose that in one such language, say Mongolian, there is no third word which simply means 'brother'. In learning English, a Mongolian speaker would learn that 'brother' is a term applied both to what he would call an *aqa* and to what he would call a *degu*. But that would not establish that 'brother' is ambiguous. What more does the Mongolian speaker learn when he learns that 'brother' is not ambiguous between 'elder brother' and 'younger brother'? If he mistakenly came to think that 'brother' was ambiguous, just what would this mistake consist in, and how might it manifest itself?

The answer, I think, is that when we learn whether or not a term is ambiguous, we learn something about the characteristic communicative intentions of speakers who use the term. It is characteristic of ambiguous predicates that speakers typically have one category or the other in mind when they use the term.[6] They intend to say something concerning one specific kind included in the extension. Moreover, in prototypical cases of ambiguity it would be regarded as odd or deviant to use the term without having one particular part of the extension in mind.[7]

[6] More accurately, they typically have in mind one category or some contextually indicated subset of a category. The need for this qualification will become evident two paragraphs further on.

[7] This oddness is manifested in dialogues like the following:

A: We are going to have some trouble with the banks.
B: Do you mean the river banks or the financial institutions?
A: Well, I hadn't thought about that. Some of each, I suppose.

There is yet another feature of prototypical ambiguous predicates which will be of considerable importance in the sections to follow. I have already said that when using ambiguous predicates speakers typically have some one part of the extension in mind, and that it is regarded as odd or deviant not to. But in some cases this provision is rather too easy to satisfy. The cases I have in mind are those in which one of the categories to be found in the total extension of the predicate is entirely included in another. For example, two distinct categories to be found in the extension of '(is an) elephant' are the class of all elephants and the class of elephants born in captivity. Typically, when speakers use the predicate they have one category or the other in mind, and it would be odd not to. Still, this hardly establishes that '(is an) elephant' is ambiguous. The reason, of course, is that the conditions specified in the previous paragraph are, so to speak, vacuously satisfied. Speakers typically have one category or the other in mind because they almost always have the larger category in mind. What we must add to fill out our characterization of prototypical ambiguous predicates is that both sorts of intentions must be common or expected. It is because it is neither common nor expected for '(is an) elephant' to be used with the intention of saying something concerning only elephants born in captivity that we do not regard this predicate as ambiguous.[8]

It is important to note that although it is odd to use an ambiguous predicate without the intention of saying something concerning one or another category included in the overall extension, it is not in the least odd to use a *non*-ambiguous predicate *with* such an intention. Indeed, it is quite common for a non-ambiguous predicate to be used with the intention of saying something concerning some subset of the full extension of the predicate. Misunderstanding in these cases is generally avoided because the speaker's intention is signalled by the context, or is made obvious in virtue of widely shared

Contrast this with:

    A: We are going to have some trouble with the parents.
    B: Do you mean the mothers or the fathers?
    A: Well, I hadn't thought about that. Some of each, I suppose.

I should note, for the record, that this condition requires the same qualification noted in the previous footnote.

[8] I suspect that this third condition is not independent of the previous pair. Indeed, when properly elaborated it might well turn out that it entails them. Still, I think there is some heuristic value in stating the three conditions separately.

background knowledge. In section 4, I will illustrate this point in some detail.

Let me bring this brief discussion of ambiguity to a close by making a pair of points. The first is that the account I have given is intended as no more that a very preliminary sketch of the features underlying our intuitive judgements of ambiguity. A full theory, plotting out the relations among ambiguity and other folk-semantic notions, would require both a more detailed account of the features I have invoked and an extended exploration of other dimensions which characterize the conceptual space of folk semantics. Doing the job properly would require a book that I very much hope someone else will write.

My second point is that if the account I have sketched is on the right track, then the notion of ambiguity ought to admit of degrees. On my account, an ambiguous predicate is one which speakers typically use with a certain sort of communicative intention, and it is regarded as odd to use the predicate without the appropriate sort of intention. But obviously typicality is a matter of degree, and some non-typical uses may be regarded as odder than others. Also, on my account, it is common or expected for a prototypical ambiguous predicate to be used with two (or more) distinct communicative intentions. And this feature, too, is obviously one that admits of degrees. In the philosophical literature there are sporadic, inconclusive debates about the ambiguity or non-ambiguity of certain philosophically important terms like 'exists' or 'sees' or 'good'.[9] A tacit and all-but-universal presupposition of these debates is that ambiguity is a property, and that having it is an all-or-nothing affair. I submit that the reason these debates are so consistently inconclusive is that this presupposition is false. Most of the philosophically pregnant terms on which they focus are neither clear cases of ambiguity nor clear cases of non-ambiguity.

3. THE LINK BETWEEN AMBIGUITY AND THE ARGUMENT FROM ANOMALOUS INTUITIONS

In the first section of this paper I reconstructed what I claimed was the best, indeed very nearly the only, argument that has been offered for the ambiguity of belief predicates. In the second section

[9] See, e.g., Wiggins (1971) and Alston (1971).

I took a closer look at just what is being claimed when a predicate is said to be ambiguous. The task of the current section is to tie the previous two together. The question I want to pose is this: if it is granted that my account of ambiguity is on the right track, why does the argument from anomalous intuitions give us any reason to think that belief predicates are ambiguous?

The Quinean argument reconstructed in section 1 is best viewed as a (putative) inference to the best explanation. The data to be explained are the anomalous intuitions: against the background of an appropriate scenario, a belief predicate can be heard or understood both as clearly applying to a certain person and as clearly not applying to that person. The sentence formed by appending the belief predicate to the person's name can be heard both as clearly true and as clearly false. The explanation offered is that the predicate and the sentence formed from it are ambiguous. But now, given our account of ambiguity, just how would the (hypothesized) fact that the predicate is ambiguous explain the anomalous intuitions?

The beginnings of an answer, I suppose, would go like this. If the predicate 'believes that p' is ambiguous, then there must be two (or more) categories in its extension, two or more different kinds of people of whom 'believes that p' is true. Moreover, it must be the case that in using the predicate speakers typically have one or the other category in mind, and that it is common or expected for speakers to have communicative intentions concerning either one. All of this simply recapitulates my account of ambiguity. Now when we process a sentence as listeners or readers, presumably part of what we do is attempt to reconstruct the communicative intentions that the speaker might have had in mind in uttering the sentence. When the sentence in question is ambiguous, we may reconstruct two (or more) possible communicative intentions. In the case at hand, we reconstruct a pair of intentions, one claiming that the believer is a member of one category in the extension of 'believes that p', the other claiming that the believer is a member of the other category. Of course, we may not reconstruct both intentions each time we hear the sentence, since it is possible for context to disambiguate by directing our attention to one interpretation or another. In the scenarios which form the backdrop for these sentences in Quine-style arguments, the believer falls into one category, but not the other. When we hear the predicate as applying to the believer, it is because we are focusing on the communicative intention involving the former category. When we hear it as not applying, it is because we are focusing on the communicative intention involving the latter category.

The account just given, needless to say, is no more than a very crude first approximation. And, pending the provision of a much more detailed and careful story, the reader is entitled to be a bit sceptical about the claim that the hypothesized ambiguity of belief predicates would indeed provide an explanation for the anomalous intuitions they evoke. If the details cannot be provided in a satisfactory way, then the argument from anomalous intuitions to the ambiguity of belief predicates will collapse, and the thesis I am defending will win by default. I am not much inclined to pursue this line of attack on the argument from anomalous intuitions, however. For I suspect that, for all its crudeness, something like the account in the previous paragraph is bound to be correct. But in conceding this I am not conceding that the argument from anomalous intuitions does in fact establish the ambiguity of belief predicates. If that argument is to succeed, it must be the case that the ambiguity hypothesis is the *best* explanation for the anomalous intuitions that belief predicates evoke. And it is just this that I propose to deny.

4. ANOTHER EXPLANATION FOR THE ANOMALOUS INTUITIONS

What was shown in the previous section was that, if we are not too fussy about the details, there is an explanation of anomalous intuitions invoking the hypothesis of ambiguity. An ambiguous predicate can be expected to evoke just the sort of intuitions that Quine's argument exploits. What I want to argue now is that non-ambiguous predicates can evoke an entirely parallel array of intuitions. The two crucial elements in the explanation of anomalous intuitions sketched in the previous section are, first, the fact that ambiguous predicates may be uttered with more than one communicative intention, and, second, the fact that hearers may reconstruct one or another of these intentions when they process sentences built from ambiguous predicates. But these are not phenomena which are restricted to ambiguous predicates. It is commonplace for a speaker to use a non-ambiguous predicate with the intention of saying something concerning a proper subset of the full extension of the term, with context and background knowledge serving to indicate just what the speaker has in mind. In other settings, the same predicate may be used with the intention of saying something involving a different proper subset. And, in still other settings, it may be used with the full extension in mind.

To see the point, let us consider the following scenario. Suppose that there is a farm owned by a rich country gentleman, Mr Moneybags. The principal business of this farm, and Mr Moneybags's great passion in life, is the raising of thoroughbred horses. Suppose, further, that Mr Moneybags's brother-in-law, Dr Darwin, has, for many years, been doing experiments on the ecology of the thoroughbred stable and the surrounding fields. He is particularly interested in the population ecology of the mice, insects, and other small animals in the area, and at the time our tale takes place he is in the final stages of an experiment which, he hopes, will support an important new theory. The central event in our scenario is a fire which breaks out in the thoroughbred stable. The fire is discovered almost immediately by the foreman, Mr Brown, who, with the assistance of various employees, succeeds in leading all the horses to safety. But the stable is destroyed and the surrounding fields are badly scorched. Many of the mice and other small creatures in and about the stable sustain serious injuries. It falls to Brown to inform Moneybags and Darwin of what has happened. When he phones Moneybags he says, 'There is a bit of bad news, Sir. There has been a fire in the stable. Fortunately, we got there in time. No animals were injured.' It seems clear that each sentence in this report can be understood as saying something true. Brown next phones Darwin and delivers a rather different report. 'There is some very bad news, Sir. The stable has been destroyed by a fire, and the fields are in pretty bad shape. Many animals were injured.' Here, too, it seems clear that each sentence in the report can be understood as saying something true. But the last sentence in the first report would appear to be logically incompatible with the last sentence in the second. How is it possible for us to hear them both as true? The answer, I think, is obvious enough. When Brown uses 'animals' in the first report he intends to say something about horses, and this intention is clear to us from the context. When Brown uses 'animals' in the second report he intends to say something about some more inclusive subset of the class of animals, a subset which includes mice and other small creatures. And this too is clear from the context.

Now it might be protested that this is not quite so clear-cut a case as we would like. So, with an eye on arguments still to come, let me add another brief example. Consider the predicate 'looks like Winston Churchill'. It is, to be sure, a somewhat vague predicate. But neither intuition nor the theory developed in section 2 would count it as ambiguous. It is a relatively easy task to construct a tale in which intuition dictates that this predicate both does and does not apply to a given person. Suppose, for example, that in an effort to build morale during World War II, a provincial city holds a Churchill look-alike contest which is won by one Robin Gump. This gentleman bears an undeniable resemblance to Churchill, though no one with a clear view of Gump would be likely to mistake him for Churchill. We can well imagine that during their deliberations one of the judges might say to the others, 'That man Gump looks like Winston Churchill. None of the others does.' And it is surely possible to understand the judge's remark as saying something true. But now suppose that the War Office has been seeking someone to serve as a stand-in for Churchill. The idea is to have someone who will make brief public appearances while the real Prime Minister is off at secret meetings. Reading about Gump in the Press, the War Office sends an official out to meet him. However, as soon as he lays eyes on Gump the official realizes that his trip has been in vain. The resemblance is not close enough; Gump just won't do. At the first opportunity, he phones his report to his superior. 'That man Gump does not look like Winston Churchill,' he says. It is plainly possible to hear this as saying something true. Once again we have a non-ambiguous predicate generating anomalous intuitions parallel to those exploited in Quine's argument. And once again the explanation is clear. The predicate at hand is being used with different communicative intentions in the two utterances, and the context makes this obvious.

What I would conclude from these two examples is that the argument from anomalous intuitions fails to establish its conclusion. That argument offers ambiguity as the best explanation for the prima facie puzzling intuitions that belief predicates can generate. But we have just seen that non-ambiguous predicates are capable of generating parallel intuitions. So, in the absence of further argument, we have no reason to think that ambiguity is the correct explanation of the anomalous intuitions. At this point in my argument, then, the issue of ambiguity is moot.

5. AN ANALYSIS OF BELIEF SENTENCES AND A PREVIEW OF COMING ATTRACTIONS

The previous four sections have been devoted to preparing the ground and clearing away the undergrowth. I now want to tackle the question of the ambiguity of belief predicates head on. The theory I will present was developed against the background of an analysis of belief sentences that I have set out in some detail in several previous publications.[10] Although my analysis plays only a minor role in the arguments that follow, it does help to tie together the various claims I will defend. So let me begin with a brief sketch of that analysis.

On my view, a sentence of the form '*S* believes that *p*' ascribes a certain sort of cognitive state to *s* and goes on to identify that state by comparing it to a hypothetical state of the ascriber. The sort of cognitive state in question is what I call a 'belief-state'. This category of cognitive state is characterized by the role it plays in an individual's overall cognitive economy. It is the function of the embedded content sentence, *p*, to indicate *which* belief-state is being ascribed. The way this works, I think, is roughly as follows. To determine which belief-state is being ascribed to *S*, we must imagine that the content sentence were to be said in earnest by the speaker in a setting akin to the one in which the belief sentence is uttered. We must then infer back to the belief-state which would cause such an utterance. The belief-state being ascribed to *S* is one which is *similar* to this one, the degree and dimensions of similarity being largely determined by the context of the utterance. So, still very roughly, my analysis of '*S* believes that *p*' might be rendered as follows:

S is in a belief-state similar to the one that would have caused my utterance had I just now uttered *p* in earnest.

Lots of bells and whistles would have to be added to this analysis if I were to attempt to defend it here. But for present purposes the brief sketch I have just given should suffice.

Let me return, now, to the ambiguity of belief predicates. The story I want to tell is a rather complicated one, since on my view

[10] See Stich (1982) and (1983), ch. 5.

some of the belief predicates that figure prominently in Quine's argument and in subsequent philosophical discussion are indeed ambiguous. The predicates I have in mind are those whose content sentences contain indefinite descriptions and certain related expressions. But, although these predicates *are* ambiguous, the ambiguity is not induced by the 'believes that' construction. Rather, I shall argue, these predicates contain ambiguous content sentences. The analysis of belief predicates sketched above leads us to expect that ambiguity in the content sentence will generally infect the belief predicate which contains it, since sincere utterances of ambiguous content sentences may have very different beliefs as their cause. Thus the ambiguity of belief predicates whose content sentences contain indefinite descriptions is no more surprising or theoretically interesting than the ambiguity of predicates like 'believes that visiting relatives can be boring' or 'believes that Sam threw a nut at Harry'.

The following section will be devoted to an explanation and defence of my view of indefinite descriptions. In the section after that I will attend to the other class of belief predicates that figure prominently in the philosophical literature, those whose content sentences have proper names or definite descriptions as subjects. My thesis there will be that these sentences are intermediate cases—neither clearly ambiguous nor clearly not.

6. THE AMBIGUITY OF INDEFINITE DESCRIPTIONS

By an indefinite description I mean an expression like 'a man' or 'an aardvark', consisting of an indefinite article followed by a noun. Since Russell, the received wisdom about indefinite articles has been that they are actually natural-language quantifiers. On this view, the sentence

An aardvark escaped from the zoo

has the logical form

(Ex) (Aardvark (x) & Escaped from the zoo (x)),

and the sentence

An aardvark bit a man

would be rendered

(Ex) (Ey) (Aardvark (x) & Man (y) & Bit (x, y)).

Now doubtless this familiar story is correct for some uses of indefinite descriptions. But in a pair of important papers Chastain (1975) and Wilson (1978) have argued convincingly that indefinite descriptions also have a quite different use. Rather than acting as quantifiers, they serve a *referential* function. Here is how Chastain makes the point:

Sentences containing indefinite descriptions are ambiguous. Sometimes 'A mosquito is in here' and its stylistic variant 'There is a mosquito in here' must be taken as asserting merely that the place is not wholly mosquito-less, but sometimes they involve an intended reference to one particular mosquito. Their disambiguation depends on how the speaker intends the context containing them to be related to other contexts.

For example, suppose that I am reading the morning newspaper and I come across the following story:

D7: #Houston, Texas, March 10 (UPI)—Dr Michael DeBakey stated at a press conference today that an artificial heart could be developed within five years. The famed Baylor University heart surgeon said that such a development would make heart transplants unnecessary.#

I then report this fact to you by saying:

D8: #A doctor in Texas claims that artificial hearts will be developed within five years.#.

Is 'a doctor' in that token of D8 a singular term? Is it possible to trace a referential connection between that expression and a particular person, such that what I said is true if and only if *that* person claimed that artificial hearts will be developed within five years? Or am I merely asserting that the class of Texas doctors claiming that artificial hearts will be developed within five years is non-empty, as the existential quantification reading of D8 would have it? In that case what I said would be true even if the news report about DeBakey were wholly erroneous and DeBakey had never made any such claim but some other doctor in Texas had, say in a private conversation, unknown to the reporter who wrote the story. Which reading is the correct one in this case? Imagine how the conversation might continue: you ask 'Who said that?' and I answer 'Dr Michael DeBakey.' Or perhaps: you say 'I can't quite believe that' and I say 'Well, it was DeBakey who said it and he ought to know. He's a famous surgeon.' Or perhaps: you say 'What's his name?' and I say, 'Michael DeBakey. Such continuations would be unintelligible on the existential quantification reading, for they presuppose that one and only one person is being said to have claimed that artificial hearts will be developed within five years; they presuppose that there is a unique referent of 'a doctor' whose name can be requested by asking 'Who?' or 'What's his name?' and who can be identified by saying 'Michael DeBakey'.[11]

As I see it, this single extended example is sufficient to establish the ambiguity of indefinite descriptions. But if the reader finds himself less ready to be convinced, Chastain's paper and Wilson's contain numerous further examples along with some acute criticism of those who deny that indefinite descriptions admit of a referential reading. For present purposes, I will take Chastain's claim to be established. What makes Chastain's ambiguity important to our current concerns is Chastain's brief observation that sentences like 'There is a mosquito in here' are often simply stylistic variants of 'A mosquito is in here'. It follows that the ambiguity of indefinite descriptions is mirrored by a parallel ambiguity in expressions of the form 'There is a *G*'. And, indeed, the passage quoted above would be equally convincing if D8 had begun 'There is a doctor in Texas who claims . . .' rather than 'A doctor in Texas claims . . .'. What is more, a completely parallel ambiguity can be found in many other constructions that are commonly taken to be natural-language equivalents of the existential quantifier. Here is Chastain again:

Sometimes the existential quantification

(3) (Ex) (x has been eating my porridge)

is a correct paraphrase of

D44: #Someone has been eating my porridge.#

and sometimes it is not, as we can see by considering

D45: #Someone has been eating my porridge. She says her name is "Goldilocks". Here she is. What are we going to do with her?#[12]

The moral that I would draw from Chastain's arguments is a simple one. English expressions that have been taken to be natural-language equivalents of the existential quantifier are commonly ambiguous. Sometimes they are indeed functioning as quantifiers, but sometimes they serve as singular terms referring to particular persons or objects. This is, I think, a genuine ambiguity, on a suitably elaborated version of the account of ambiguity sketched earlier. When using indefinite descriptions and related expressions, speakers typically intend one reading or the other and they expect

---

[11] Chastain (1975), pp. 212–13. [12] Ibid., p. 224.

other speakers to do so as well. When an ambiguous indefinite description occurs in the content sentence of a belief predicate, it will typically render the predicate itself ambiguous. Thus the belief predicates in (1) and (2), in section 1, are indeed ambiguous, and the anomalous intuitions we have about them can be traced to this ambiguity. But it is the embedded sentence not the 'believes that' construction that induces the ambiguity. So the fact that (1) and (2) can be heard as both true and false lends no support to the thesis that belief sentences are systematically ambiguous.

7. BELIEF PREDICATES CONTAINING PROPER NAMES OR DEFINITE DESCRIPTIONS

In this section I want to consider belief predicates of the form

(8) . . . believes that n is F,

where n is replaced by a proper name or definite description, and 'is F' is replaced by an unambiguous predicate. Are these belief predicates systematically ambiguous?[13] This question has all too often been conflated with the very different question of whether these belief predicates apply, when they do, in virtue of different kinds of beliefs. So let me begin by pulling these two issues apart.

It is agreed on all sides, or in any event it should be, that beliefs and the people who hold them can be categorized into a variety of different classes and kinds, some of which are interesting and some of which are not. Thus, for example, some beliefs are true and some are false; some are based on adequate evidence and some are not; some beliefs give their holders great solace; some cause enormous anguish; and some were first acquired on a Thursday. It should also be agreed on all sides that in the extension of a belief predicate like (8) there will often be people to whom the predicate applies in virtue of beliefs of different kinds. The predicate

[13] There are some writers who have taken Donnellan's referential/attributive distinction (see Donnellan (1966)) to mark an ambiguity in definite descriptions roughly parallel to the ambiguity Chastain finds in indefinite descriptions. Donnellan himself resists this construal of the distinction, and I share this scepticism. However, if a convincing case can be made for the ambiguity of definite descriptions, then belief predicates like (8) with n replaced by a definite description might be treated along the lines sketched in the previous section. Hornsby (1977) explores such a view, though she also endorses the thesis that the 'believes that' construction induces a systematic ambiguity.

(9) . . . believes that Plato's teacher was wise,

for example, may be true of me in virtue of a belief acquired on good evidence and on a Thursday, while it may be true of someone else in virtue of a belief acquired on bad evidence and on a Saturday. The fact that predicates like (8) may be true of people in virtue of different kinds of beliefs does not, of course, establish that these predicates are systematically ambiguous. No one would suggest that (9) is ambiguous because my belief that Plato's teacher was wise was acquired on a Thursday, while yours was acquired on some other day of the week. If the account of ambiguity developed earlier is on the right track, then for (9) to be ambiguous in this way it would have to be the case that speakers using (9) typically had in mind either the category of Thursday-acquired beliefs or the category of non-Thursday-acquired beliefs; it would have to be considered odd to use the predicate without intending one or the other of these categories (or some subset of one or the other of them); and both sorts of intentions would have to be common or expected. All of this is clearly false. So it is not surprising that no one takes (9) to be ambiguous between Thursday-acquired and non-Thursday-acquired beliefs.

There are, however, other distinctions to be drawn in the extensions of predicates like (8). And some of those distinctions have tempted philosophers to think that these belief predicates are ambiguous. Unfortunately, the people who are so tempted are generally not terribly explicit about the exact nature of the distinction marked by the putative ambiguity, and there is reason to think that different writers have different distinctions in mind. This situation makes it all but impossible to offer a conclusive argument against the ambiguity thesis. Putative ambiguities have to be considered one at a time. What I propose to do here is to look at a few variations on one popular idea for drawing distinctions between different categories of beliefs and believers to see if it will sustain the view that sentences like (8) are systematically ambiguous.

A distinction that looms large in the literature turns on whether the believer himself would agree that the belief predicate in question is true of him. This distinction often plays a central role when the putative ambiguity of belief sentences is being illustrated. In our Quine-style scenario in section 1, for example, the most salient difference between (3), on the one hand, and (4) and (5), on the other, was that, at the time he attacked Slewth, Goodman would have agreed with (3) and vigorously disagreed with (4) and (5). Since what is important here is that the believer would agree that his belief can be characterized with the very words that occur in the belief predicate, it might be tempting to call this category of beliefs *de dicto*.[14] Actually, I know of no philosopher who would seriously accept the characterization of the *de dicto* category that I have just given. For that characterization is language-bound, and no one wants to say that Pierre's belief that Plato's teacher was wise cannot be *de dicto* simply because Pierre, who speaks no English, does not agree that the predicate 'believes that Plato's teacher was wise' is true of him. It is enough if he would agree that the French translation of that predicate applies to him.

Let me try to say all this a bit more carefully. The idea before us is that the extension of (9), the class of people to whom this predicate truly applies, can be divided into two categories. One of these categories includes just those people who would agree[15] that (9), or some translation of it into a language they understand is true of them. These are the people who believe *de dicto* that Plato's teacher was wise. Further, it is urged that (9) is ambiguous, since sometimes it is used with the intention of saying that the person in question is a *de dicto* believer that Plato's teacher was wise, and sometimes it is not.

There is one crucial point which the view I have just sketched leaves unspecified. If (9) sometimes means 'believes *de dicto* that Plato's teacher was wise', what does it mean the rest of the time? Or, to put the question in terms more compatible with the account of ambiguity developed earlier, if one category in the extension of (9) is the class of *de dicto* believers that Plato's teacher was wise, what is the other category? The most obvious answer is that the other category is just the complement class in the extension of the predicate—the class of people of whom (9) is true but who would not agree that 'believes that Plato's teacher was wise' (or its translation into their language) applies to them. This class would, I suppose, include those first-year philosophy undergraduates who

---

[14] I have considerable sympathy with Devitt's suggestion that we simply renounce the terms '*de dicto*' and '*de re*' when talking about belief. But one cannot grind all one's axes at once.

[15] Under normal circumstances, if they were inclined to be honest, etc. Let's not quibble.

have read enough to be impressed by Socrates' wisdom, but not enough to realize that he was Plato's teacher. On this way of distinguishing categories in the extension of belief predicates, our friend Goodman in section 1 would be included in the *de dicto* extension of 'believes that Slewth was burgling the safe' (see (3)). Goodman is also to be found in the extensions of the predicates 'believed that the owner of the factory was burgling the safe' and 'believed that Peter Rich was burgling the safe' (see (4) and (5)), but not in the *de dicto* part of these extensions.

We now have a reasonably clear proposal before us. Belief predicates, it is claimed, are systematically ambiguous between the *de dicto* and the non-*de dicto* readings. It is also reasonably clear that this proposal is false. If belief predicates were systematically ambiguous in this way, then assuming that my earlier account of ambiguity is on the right track, it would have to be the case that speakers have one sub-extension or the other in mind when they use belief predicates, and that it is regarded as odd or deviant not to. But this seems clearly wrong. To see the point, consider the following dialogue:

Adams: Have you heard the news? The trustees have just appointed Greely dean of the college.
Brown: They may come to regret that decision.
A: Oh, why is that?
B: Smith believes that our new dean has been stealing university money.

If the ambiguity thesis as currently construed were correct, it would be odd for Brown to say what he did in the last line of the dialogue without specifically intending either the *de dicto* or the non-*de dicto* category (or some subset of one of these). What this amounts to, in the case at hand, is that it would be odd for Brown to say what he did without having some view on whether Smith is aware that Greely is the new dean. But this, surely, is just wrong. Brown may have no idea whether Smith believes that Greely is the new dean and thus he may have no idea whether Smith would agree that the belief predicate Brown invokes is true of him. It is commonplace, and not in the least odd or deviant, for speakers to use belief predicates without knowing whether the believer falls into the *de dicto* or the non-*de dicto* category, and without intending to commit themselves one way or the other. It follows that belief predicates are not ambiguous in the way currently under consideration.

There is, however, a rather different way in which the category of *de dicto* believers might be thought to be associated with a systematic ambiguity of belief predicates. In the proposal just rejected, belief predicates were claimed to be ambiguous between the *de dicto* category and its complement class within the extension. It might instead be suggested that the ambiguity is between the *de dicto* category and the *full* extension of the predicate, much as 'corn' is ambiguous between 'maize' and 'edible grain'. This proposal is immune from the sort of critique mounted against the previous one. The strategy there was to construct a case in which the speaker intended to locate the believer in the extension of a belief predicate and had no sub-extension in mind. Such cases will not count as counter-examples to the ambiguity thesis as currently construed, since one of the two categories on which the alleged ambiguity turns is the full extension of the predicate. More generally, when one of the two categories involved in an alleged ambiguity is the full extension, the 'oddness' condition in our account of ambiguity will typically be vacuously satisfied. It is almost sure to be odd to use a predicate with the communicative intention of locating the object in question in some category which is not included in the overall extension of that predicate. It follows that, in cases where the alleged ambiguity is of the full-extension-versus-subset variety, the final condition in our account of ambiguity must decide the issue. We have a genuine ambiguity to the extent that it is common or expected for speakers to have the subset in question in mind when they use the predicate.

Well, to what extent is this condition satisfied by belief predicates? The answer, I am afraid, is that I just do not know. Nor do I know of any easy way of finding out. It is surely the case that *sometimes* when speakers use belief predicates like (8) they intend to ascribe a belief which the believer himself would agree he has. But this hardly establishes that it is a common practice generating an appropriately strong set of expectations. To see the point, we need only recall our discussion of predicates like 'looks like Churchill'. *Sometimes* people use this predicate with the intention of ascribing to the person in question a resemblance so close that he might successfully serve as Churchill's stand-in. And when a speaker does have this intention in mind it is generally obvious enough to his audience. But in reconstructing the speaker's intention, the audience does not rely on any knowledge that the predicate is commonly used in this way. They could not, since it is not commonly used in this way. What they do instead is to infer what the speaker has in mind from the complex cues provided by the context. Similarly, it might be urged that when an audience realizes that a speaker is using a belief predicate with the intention of ascribing a *de dicto* belief, they do so by exploiting complex contextual cues rather than by relying on prior knowledge that such intentions are common and to be expected. My guess here, and it is really little more than a guess, is that the intention to ascribe *de dicto* beliefs is rather more common, and is known to be rather more common, than the intention to ascribe similarity of looks adequate for a stand-in. To the extent that people have such knowledge, they no doubt exploit it along with the information provided by contextual cues in reconstructing the communicative intentions of the speaker. If this is right, then predicates like (8) are more ambiguous than 'looks like Churchill'. But, and here I am guessing again, the practice of ascribing *de dicto* beliefs with predicates like (8) is not nearly so commonplace as the practice of using 'salt' to say something about table salt, or the practice of using 'corn' to say something about maize. If this is right, then predicates like (8) are less ambiguous than 'salt' and 'corn' and other paradigm cases of ambiguous predicates like 'bank' and 'nut'.

Are belief predicates ambiguous? If my speculations are anywhere close to the mark, then the answer is that there is no answer. They are, or at least some of them are, intermediate cases. Moreover, the question turns out to be not a terribly interesting one. Of much more interest would be a careful taxonomy of the different kinds of beliefs that people sometimes intend to ascribe with belief predicates, and a systematic account of how prior expectations and contextual cues combine in allowing them to convey their intentions to their audience. I think that there is much insight into these matters to be found in the philosophical literature on these questions, even though most writers in this area took themselves to be concerned with other, darker, questions.[16]

---

[16] This paper is my third effort to get straight on these matters. The first was an unpublished paper, co-authored with D. C. Dennett, and read to a conference at Bristol University in 1978. The second was ch. 6 of Stich (1983), from which much of sections 1 and 3 of the present paper are borrowed. Even before that book appeared,

BIBLIOGRAPHY

Alston, W. (1971) 'How Does One Tell Whether a Word Has One, Several or Many Senses?' in D. Steinberg and L. Jakobovits (edd.), *Semantics* (Cambridge UP).

Armstrong, D. M. (1973) *Belief, Truth and Knowledge* (Cambridge UP).

Chastain, C. (1975) 'Reference and Context', in K. Gunderson (ed.), *Minnesota Studies in the Philosophy of Science*, Vol. 7 (University of Minn. Press).

Devitt, M. (1984) 'Thoughts and Their Ascription', in P. French, T. Uehling, and H. Wettstein (edd.), *Midwest Studies in Philosophy*, Vol. 9 (University of Minn. Press).

Donnellan, K. (1966) 'Reference and Definite Descriptions', *Philosophical Review*, 75.

Grandy, R. (1973) 'Reference, Meaning and Belief', *Journal of Philosophy*, 70.

Hintikka, J. (1962) *Knowledge and Belief* (Cornell UP).

—— (1967) 'Individuals, Possible Worlds and Epistemic Logic', *Nous*, 1.

—— (1970) 'Objects of Knowledge and Belief: Acquaintances and Public Figures', *Journal of Philosophy*, 67.

Hornsby, J. (1977) 'Singular Terms in Contexts of Propositional Attitudes', *Mind*, 86.

Kaplan, D. (1968) 'Quantifying In', *Synthese*, 19.

Quine, W. (1956) 'Quantifiers and Propositional Attitudes', *Journal of Philosophy*, 53.

Rey, G. (forthcoming) 'Concepts and Stereotypes', *Cognition*.

Sellars, W. F. (1968) 'Some Problems about Belief', *Synthese*, 19.

Smith, E., and Medin, D. (1981) *Concepts and Categories* (Harvard UP).

Sosa, E. (1970) 'Propositional Attitudes *de Dictu* and *de Re*', *Journal of Philosophy*, 67.

a number of people, most notably William Lycan and Brian Haugh, had badgered me into believing that I hadn't got things quite right.

The present paper was written while I was a Fellow at the Center for Advanced Study in the Behavioral Sciences in Stanford, Ca. I am grateful for financial support provided by the Andrew Mellon Foundation and the National Endowment for the Humanities. Kent Bach, Michael Devitt, Ray Jackendoff, William Lycan, Julius Moravcsik, Christopher Peacocke, Elizabeth Traugott, and William Wang have helped with examples, advice and criticism. I don't think any of them believes a word of it, but I am grateful for their help.

While I was making final revisions I had occasion to reread Grandy's insightful paper (1973), in which he suggests, albeit very briefly, a view of belief sentences not unlike the one elaborated here (cf. p. 447). It is entirely possible that the seeds of my account of belief were planted when I first read Grandy's paper, more than a decade ago. If there is anything in this paper that he agrees with, he has a clear claim to priority.

Stich, S. P. (1982) 'On the Ascription of Content', in A. Woodfield (ed.), *Thought and Object* (Oxford UP).

—— (1983) *From Folk Psychology to Cognitive Science: The Case Against Belief* (MIT Press).

Wallace, J. (1972) 'Belief and Satisfaction', *Nous*, 4.

Wiggins, D. (1971) 'On Sentence Sense, Word Sense and Differences of Word Sense. Towards a Philosophical Theory of Dictionaries', in D. Steinberg and L. Jakobovits (edd.), *Semantics* (Cambridge UP).

Wilson, G. (1978) 'On Definite and Indefinite Descriptions', *Philosopical Review*, 87.

CHAPTER 7

THE MANUFACTURE OF BELIEF

RADU J. BOGDAN

I. INTRODUCTION

The beginning of the story is familiar enough. A belief is a mental form with a propositional content, that is, a formal structure of some complexity which encodes some meaningful information that such and such is so and so. This is the sense in which a belief is a mental representation. A belief is also a mental representation with some cognitive or behavioural business. So we can think of belief as a function *from* a content-encoding mental form *to* a cognitive or behavioural role. Such a characterization fits the currently standard notion of belief.

But we have a serious problem here. The problem is that the standard notion of belief is incomplete and inadequate. It accounts for much less than it should. As a result, it projects the wrong picture of belief as a *mental* phenomenon. If belief is thought of as a function from content to role, then understanding belief amounts to understanding the nature of this function, which in turn means understanding the constraints which shape it. What the standard notion of belief fails to identify and explain are precisely the conditions which shape the belief function, that is, the conditions in which a content-encoding mental form comes to play a cognitive or behavioural role and thus becomes a belief. This, obviously, is a very critical failure, for the very essence of belief, that of being a function from mental representation to causal role in cognition and behaviour, is left totally unexplained. Nor is the failure much noticed, let alone deplored. It is standard procedure in current literature on belief to say that a belief is a representation-in-a role without any thought being given to how the two aspects, representation and role, come together in the first place. When we ask, what is it about a mental representation that makes it a belief?, the standard answer is, its playing a role. But that is to beg the question.

For, again, what I am asking is, what is it about a mental representation that makes it play a role in the first place?

This paper is not going to answer that question, certainly not the whole question. But it is meant to go some way towards answering it. The basic idea is this. What is missing from the standard notion of belief is an essential ingredient of mental content, namely, the specific information that mental representations must encode in order to animate the organism's cognition and behaviour and thus becomes beliefs. This, I argue, is going to be an occurrently and incrementally manufactured information. The constraints on this form of information, if they contribute to a representation's becoming a belief, are *ipso facto* going to be constraints on the very function from mental representation to cognitive/behavioural role, the function we associate with belief as a mental phenomenon. That is what the next section is going to establish. But then, if we reflect on the mental nature of these information-inspired constraints on belief, we are bound to conclude that belief is very different from what the standard story tells us it is. This is when, in sections 3 and 4, our story turns less than familiar. For, if the belief function maps occurrently and incrementally formed information onto an appropriate role, then belief is neither a mere disposition, nor an enduring state of some sort, let alone a mere stored representation. Belief draws on these aspects but is reducible to none of them. Belief is occurrently manufactured out of a number of mental dimensions at a central rather than modular level. To have a belief is to manufacture or fix it. This is the sense in which belief is a type of mental performance. Such a notion of belief emerges if we think straight and hard about how mental representations convey the information which drives an organism's cognition and behaviour.

2. THE MISSION DIMENSION

The problem

The standard notion, as we saw, construes belief as a mental representation which plays a cognitive or behavioural role. The mental representation in turn is construed as a syntactic form of some sort, in some code, which represents or refers to some fact or state of affairs. The form, in other words, has an intentional content. Concepts, meanings, recognition patterns, stereotypes, and the like are the ingredients and shapers of intentional contents.

Thus, for example, if a mental representation is a thought-expressing sentence in English, then its form is the grammatical/logical structure of the sentence, and the intentional content the thought or meaning expressed. The intentional content of a (propositional) representation is different from the representation's semantic co-ordinates. The latter determine what (in the world) makes a representation true, the former what (in the mind) makes a representation encode a thought, a meaning, a conceptual structure, or the like. I construe our 'intentional programme' as a sort of basic and minimal conceptual schematism which (in a Kantian way) organizes the syntactic input. Such a programme computes meaning, as conceptual content, in a rigid, automatic, and predetermined way. Many philosophers think that the semantic co-ordinates are also needed to type-individuate a belief. I am going to set this issue on one side since, no matter how solved, it adds nothing to the characterization of belief as a *mental* phenomenon, which is what we are interested in here. There are, therefore, three dimensions to the standard notion of belief: a syntactic form, s, an intentional content or meaning, m, and a cognitive or behavioural role, r. Belief, we saw, can be conceptualized as a function from a mental representation to a role. To put it schematically: BEL = Rep $(s,m) \rightarrow (r)$.

An attractively appropriate metaphor for this standard notion of belief is the idea that a belief is a 'map by which we steer'.[1] A map, we can say, is a graphic structure meant to represent a certain territory. It has only syntactic form and, given its purpose, it is meant to have an intentional content, i.e. to represent (be about) something. That is all a map is. The critical problem is: how is the map going to do the steering? How, in particular, is a mental map going to do its cognitive or behavioural steering?

The underlying assumptions behind behind the standard view are (1) that the constraints on Rep(s,m) are the only basic constraints on the mental *content* of the belief function involved, and (2) that additional mental attitudes, such as plans, desires, habits, even other beliefs, will channel that content into the appropriate cognitive or behavioural roles it can play. This is to say that *what* one

[1] The full quotation is 'A belief of the primary sort is a map of a neighbouring space by which we steer', from F. Ramsey, *The Foundations of Mathematics* (1931), p. 238. D. M. Armstrong, among others, has articulated this metaphor in some detail in his *Belief, Truth and Knowledge* (Cambridge UP, 1973).

believes is a meaning or intentional content encoded in some formal structure of some sort; and that one's *believing* consists in that content being harnessed to do some job by other mental attitudes and behavioural tendencies.

But this is not going to work. There are many representations we perceive or remember or entertain or infer which fail to become beliefs, although both their syntactic structure and their intentional content are fully computed. We know of cases when, overhearing an isolated sentence, we can compute its syntactic form and basic meaning but that is all we can do. We cannot place it in a context, cannot ascertain its actual aboutness and, most importantly, cannot tell what message it conveys. To say that such representations fail to become beliefs because they fail to engage other mental attitudes is to beg again the original question—a question which can now be restated as: why do those representations fail to engage other attitudes? Suppose it is true, as many philosophers think, that a mental representation becomes a belief by attitudinal integration with other beliefs, plans, and intentions, among other things. My question is, what triggers and motivates such integration? The question asked before, what is it about a mental representation that makes it a belief?, now becomes, what is it about a mental representation that makes other attitudes and behavioural programmes converge on, and interact with, it? Imagine the existing mental attitudes being some sort of 'readers' of incoming representations, programmed to look for some properties which make those representations candidates for belief. What are those attitudes looking for? It cannot be only s and m. This means that the formal and intentional dimensions cannot fully characterize a belief content. It looks as if there must be something more to a content to attract and engage other mental attitudes so that that content moves into a role position and acquires a doxastic status.

The map metaphor can provide a clue. A map is not going to do the steering just by being a map, i.e. a $\text{Rep}(s)$. Nor is it going to do the steering just by being made, or meant, to represent some territory and thus guide the steering, i.e. by being a $\text{Rep}(s,m)$. Something more is needed. Not, trivially, a map reader but, rather, a traveller who knows where he is and where he is going, besides having some more specific objectives and expectations. It takes this locational information to make the map guide the steering.

You may think that I am adding to our picture of cognition some sort of homunculus which reads the incoming Rep(s,m) for some specific information, given its instructions, objectives, and available data, in the way our traveller reads the map for specific information which will steer his path, given his instructions, objectives, and available data. In a way I am, although not exactly in this form.[2] But do not, for one moment, believe that this is an arbitrary move, for it is continuous and consistent with other, apparently more natural, hypotheses about cognition. How do you think s and m are established? Take the perceptual input. In itself it is just an aggregation of physical properties. Is there not, in the vision module, a computing homunculus which 'reads' into (or assigns to) the perceptual input specific formal properties—i.e., which maps the input on to an appropriate visual Rep(s)? Or do we not say, when the language module is involved, that there is a grammar-computing homunculus which reads into (or assigns to) collection of noises a specific grammatical structure? And when concepts and other intentional constraints are added, do we not say (or rather mean) that there is an intentional homunculus which reads into (or assigns to) an apropriate Rep(s) a specific meaning structure, thus mapping the former on to a Rep(s,m)? So, if it takes a syntactic and then an intentional homunculus (or reader) to construct a mental map or representation, first as a formal structure and then as an intentional structure, would it not be equally natural to assume that it took another information-computing sort of humunculus (or reader), perhaps in different cognitive conditions, to assign to (or read into) a Rep(s,m) some locational information, and thus pave the way for the Rep(s,m) to take on a role and become a belief? If, in the map metaphor, it takes some locational information to make a map capable of and useful for steering, it is fair to assume that a mental analogue of some such locational information must be read into a mental Rep(s,m) in order to get the latter to play a steering role.

It is this analogue of locational information which is missing, as a dimension of content, from the standard notion of belief. The mental content that gets mapped on to a role is not to be characterized merely as Rep(s,m), for in that case we cannot explain the mapping, but rather (at the least) as Rep($s,m,\square$), where $\square$ is the slot for the analogue of the locational information. The adequate

[2] I construe a homunculus or reader as a metaphoric 'personalization' of an appropriate programme. No genuine reification is meant.

characterization of belief as a function from a mentally represented content to a cognitive-behavioural role, then, is going to be BEL = $\text{Rep}(s,m,\square) \rightarrow (r)$. The constraints on $\square$ are naturally going to be additional and much-needed constraints on the belief function, on its content side. That is what I am going to show next. Once that is done, reflection on how the mind realizes the constraints on $\square$ shows that $\square$, as an essential ingredient of belief content, is manufactured only in the central mind, as a matter of occurrent performance. Belief, then, must inherit these features. That is, it must be manufactured centrally and occurrently because that is how the analogue of the locational information a belief encodes is manufactured and because there is no belief without such information. It is as simple as that. In other words, if one is serious about the idea that a belief represents information, then one has to look at the conditions in which such information is fixed. One has *also* to free oneself of the admittedly irresistible prejudice that information is (no more than) what a representation represents, or refers to, or is about (that is, an intentional or semantic content). When one has made these two steps, one is bound to conclude that belief tracks information, not merely the form and the intentional content of the representation carrying that information. One must then conclude that the manufacture of belief is parasitic on the manufacture of the information the belief encodes.

That is what I am going to argue. I begin with a handy illustration.

A story

Babeau and Babette come home and learn that, this time, Pusha has destroyed the cassette of Bruckner's Seventh Symphony. (Pusha hates Bruckner's music and anything else connected with interminable and fuzzy Teutonic romanticism.) Let us suppose that the following aspects are essentially the same for Babeau and Babette: causing event (Pusha mangling the Bruckner cassette); sensory input about it; formal and intentional computations of all sorts; hence the representational output $\text{Rep}(s,m)$ to the effect that Pusha has destroyed the Bruckner cassette; desire (to hear the newly bought cassette). Nevertheless, their reactions to the news are different. Babeau is relieved and goes after another cassette, Babette is rather angry and goes after Pusha. The difference in their reactions must originate among other factors in the beliefs they have formed. For this to happen, Babeau and Babette must have extracted different pieces of information from the same input representation Rep(s,m) to the effect that Pusha has destroyed the Bruckner cassette. Shaped by what they already knew and did not know, their informational expectations were different. Indeed, Babeau knew in advance that Pusha had destroyed a classical-music cassette but did not know which one, whereas Babette only knew that Pusha had destroyed something but did not know what. The same input representation conveyed different information to Babette and Babeau—or, more precisely, different increments in information. Their beliefs must, in some sense, have been shaped by these increments. Let us see how.

The parameters

The central notion is that of *incremental information*. It is what the earlier symbol □ stood for. Let us now abbreviate it as CINF. I construe CINF as an intrinsic part of mental content. I have argued for this elsewhere.[3] Since, by examples like the one above, CINF can be shown to be instrumental in driving cognition and behaviour by causing further beliefs, intentions, inferences, and actions, among other things, it is fair to assume that it operates as part of the belief content. There are, furthermore, a number of parameters that shape CINF for a believer in a given cognitive context. These parameters, as constraints on CINF, can then be construed as constraints on belief as well. I will identify only a few such parameters, enough to serve the cause of my overall argument.

Trivial as it may seem, an initial parameter is the *theme* of one's current cognition in a given context. The reason the theme matters is that more representations reach us than we can actively consider and treat as beliefs. We can, for example, monitor some perceptual input while actively focusing on a particular train of thoughts. The information the latter carry is going to be the current theme of our cognition. Again, at any moment in our story, Babeau and Babette have to handle various sorts of representations, yet (we assume) only those concerned with Pusha's misdeeds constitute their current theme. A theme, obviously, delineates an area of interest and attention. In so doing, it marks a path of relevant informational

[3] See R. J. Bogdan, 'Mind, Content and Information', forthcoming in *Synthese*. That paper says more about my notion of incremental information, its precedents (particularly in F. Dretske's work), its competitors, its psychological reality, and its philosophical implications. So it is in fact a companion paper to this one.

continuity as well as the boundaries of potential incrementation and revision. Believing must emerge from within a theme if, as earlier anticipated, belief is not any available representation but rather one 'read' for specific information on which other mental resources (attitudes, inferences, etc.) converge.

The next parameter we want to consider may be called the *issue* parameter. It defines what is informationally at stake in a given context, relative to a theme. In our story, the issue was a specific uncertainty concerning Pusha's doings. Many of our beliefs are formed as a result of removing uncertainties. But an issue may be something different from an uncertainty. It may be a problem to be solved, a question to be answered, a decision to be made, a plan to be formulated, and so on. I would argue that most if not all of our beliefs are issue-bound, in some sense or another. This is because, I think, beliefs are formed or activated in a matrix of thoughts, inferences, intentions, and other processes and attitudes, and those in turn are formed, activated, and brought together in contexts of problem-solving, deciding, or acting, hence, when the organism faces some issue.

This brings us to the next parameter. A target belief about an issue is formed when other beliefs and representations are premised as *given information* in a certain context. This parameter specifies the background knowledge (whatever its source) deemed relevant to the issue in question. A further parameter to consider is the following. When something is at issue, the mind not only summons relevant beliefs to act as given information but also, relative to them and other constraints, projects a number of alternative candidates for the solution. Let us call this the *projection* parameter. It plays a role in our understanding of belief. Typically, one believes something *as opposed to something else*. The projection parameter governs the generation, explicit or not, of such contrasting alternatives. We may assume that the projection parameter works in tandem with some *evaluation* parameter which characterizes the work of some plausibility or likelihood metric. The latter provides standards against which both projected alternatives and the candidate accepted are measured with respect to plausibility and likelihood. If a candidate for a solution to an issue is deemed implausible or unlikely, the organism may be instructed to suspend belief, search for additional information, or start all over again. The projection and evaluation parameters become evident in contexts where we have to, or want to, quantify the strength of our beliefs by specifying both stakes and alternatives. Scepticism, for example, provides such a context.

Finally, two more parameters. The *new information* specifies the increment which is going to remove an uncertainty, answer a question, or, in general, settle the issue at hand. The new information does not have to be really new; it needs only to be additional information relative to what is available in the context. Once accepted, the new information is integrated into the given information. The result can be called *integrated information*. The updating of our beliefs takes this form of incremental integration. Most if not all of our beliefs are manufactured incrementally in the process of expanding, reconfirming, or revising our knowledge.

Even when we examine and question existing beliefs, with apparently no new information involved, I still want to claim that the framework in which we do so is incremental in the sense that it is governed by parameters like those introduced here. Suppose I ask myself, about an existing belief of mine, 'Do I believe that P?' Note what I am doing. By hypothesis, since it is an existing belief, P is part of my pool of given information, say, a memory item. The theme now is: worry about an existing belief. Specific issue: is P true? I look everywhere in memory for additional given information X. Relative to X and an appropriate evaluation metric I project as relevant the contrasting alternatives P and not-P. After some cogitating, the answer comes in the form of the increment: 'P is true.' As a result, P is returned to doxastic favour and confined again to memory. The framework of this belief fixation is incremental, first, because for a moment 'P is true' was in doubt, therefore its addition to the given information is incremental; and second, because its very addition to and reincorporation into the existing knowledge base proceeded relative to a number of parameters of incrementation. The question 'Is P true?' is, after all, a request for information ('Yes' or 'No'), and, as shown, the way to provide the information and answer the question is incremental. Belief examination, revision, or reconfirmation is as incremental as belief acquisition. All are cases of belief fixation.

There may be other, more distant, parameters which play a role in determining CINF, hence what is believed, but I will stop here. My purpose is not to provide an exhaustive analysis of CINF, let alone of belief content, but rather to show that the presence of something like CINF in a belief content suggests that the mental-type identity of belief be construed as a sort of central performance or occurrent manufacture. But first let us take stock of our parameters. The first two delineate the 'cognitive ambience' of believing:

(A) (*i*) theme: what is attended to, area of interest
     (*ii*) issue: uncertainty, problem to be solved, etc.

The next parameters specify the mental moves which are being made in order to handle, informationally, the issue in question, moves which amount to the forming and positioning of the appropriate blocks of information:

  (*iii*) given information: what is selected and held as fixed
  (*iv*) projected alternatives: candidates for the new information
  (*v*) evaluation metric: measuring the candidates for plausibility
  (*vi*) the new information
  (*vii*) integrated information: updating the given with the new information

Many parameters are often valued by default, automatically. The valuation may to a large extent be unconscious. We typically become aware of it only if something goes wrong or is surprising or something of the sort. I take quite seriously the parallel between the fixation of incremental information, on the one hand, and the syntactic computation of grammatical structure and the intentional computation of meaning, on the other hand. If we are now accustomed to the notion that the latter are unconscious, inaccessible to ordinary intuition, and posited as explanatory constructs, we should treat in the same way more central processes and outputs involving information and mental attitudes. This means, pre-emptively, that ordinary, as well as standard philosophical, intuitions have no privileged access to such phenomena as the fixation of information and belief, nor do they explain them very well.

The content of a belief is manufactured in an incremental environment like that described in (A). Let us motivate this by bringing theory and example together. Babeau was credited with coming to believe that Pusha has destroyed a Bruckner cassette.

This is an incremental belief whose very informal analysis might look liks this:

(B) Theme: Pusha's misdeeds
  Given: Pusha has destroyed a classical-music cassette
  Issue: uncertainty: which cassette?
  Projected: (i) Wagner's *Tristan?* (ii) Bruckner's Fifth? (iii) Satie?
  Evaluation: (i) likely, (ii) likely, (iii) certainly not
  New: Bruckner's Seventh
  Integrated: Pusha has destroyed a cassette of Bruckner's Seventh.

Babette's story, on the other hand, is this:

(C) Theme: Pusha's misdeeds
  Given: Pusha has destroyed something
  Issue: uncertainty: what something?
  Projected: (i) cassette? (ii) bottle of wine? (iii) book?
  Evaluation: (i) likely, (ii) very likely, (iii) likely
  New: cassette of Bruckner's Seventh Symphony
  Integrated: Pusha has destroyed a cassette of Bruckner's Seventh Symphony.

In what follows, my working notion of information is CINF, which is what is implicitly characterized by (A) and illustrated by (B) and (C). No other notion of information is intended or assumed. As we shall see in a moment, CINF does approximate a rather standard notion of information.

Belief and information

The essence of CINF is (at the least) the joint product of the distance or gap between the given and the integrated information *and* the number of alternatives the increment or new information must remove to bridge that initial distance or gap. In other words, one's overall informational gain in a given situation of incrementation is measured by what one needs to know in order to handle the issue one is facing, relative to what one knows already and what one expects. In our story the informational gains of Babeau and Babette are quite different, even though they end up with the same integrated information. For their informational starting points are different. This is why neither the representation of the integrated information nor that of the new information can, *by itself*, characterize the informational gain, CINF, that Babeau and Babette end up with.

To generalize a little, think of the standard notion of information as reduction of uncertainty by elimination of competing alternatives. This is the notion that CINF approximates. The point I am making is that neither an incoming message (corresponding to our new information) nor what the message updates, an existing body of knowledge (corresponding to our integrated information), can fully characterize the incremental information it helps articulate. To specify that incremental information we have to go beyond the message and what it updates, that is, to an initial uncertainty, to what was expected to remove that uncertainty, and so on. The determination of information is a multi-dimensional affair which transcends its individual carriers. Particular mental representations are such carriers. An account of their intrinsic properties is not sufficient to characterize the information those representations carry.

If belief tracks information, it must track such a multi-dimensional configuration of representations as is required to specify CINF. In other words, if CINF is part of what is believed, the belief equation is $BEL = Rep(s,m,CINF) \rightarrow (r)$. Now why would belief track information? Quite honestly, the project of this paper is not to answer this question but rather to exploit its presupposition, namely, that belief tracks information. In other words, my project here has the following conditional format: if belief tracks information, *then* (I want to show) it tracks incremental information and does so occurrently. So the scope of my project extends only to the consequent of this conditional. But I want to touch on the antecedent.

Two intuitive considerations have already been made. One is that we do think of information when we think of belief, whatever the final analysis of the two concepts is going to be. It will be hard to think that the notion of belief content does not have room for the notion of information. One may of course assimilate information to some other dimensions, such as meaning or reference. I shall come to this in a moment. The other intuitive consideration exploits the parallel between belief and information. I have earlier shown how some parameters of incremental information fit our notion of belief. This is particularly obvious if we attend to the ways in which we explicitly and deliberately form and use beliefs, from ordinary to scientific. A standard case, much studied in inductive logic and philosophy of science, is that of hypothesis formation, which is a case of belief formation. Forming a hypothesis takes place relative to a body of given information (evidence, theory, other hypotheses) and competing candidates (hypotheses). An evaluation metric is summoned to measure the evidential support, informativeness, explanatory power, and other qualities of the candidates. Once formed, a hypothesis can be integrated into the body of accepted hypotheses. And so on. Of all the constitutive components of a belief content, i.e. syntactic form, meaning, information, it must be the shaping of information that this model of hypothesis formation mirrors.

In ordinary life the process of belief formation is more implicit. Some of the parameters are valued by default. But the point remains that the process is more likely to track the shaping of information than that of syntactic form, semantic aboutness, or meaning. Consider perceptual belief (meaning belief that owes a lot to perception, *not* belief fixed within, say, the vision module, for there is no such thing). Imagine yourself seeing something that can be represented as: 'There is an alligator down the corridor'. Think now of how your (reluctant and horrified) doxastic attitude is going to engage this representation, *after* you have made syntactic and intentional sense of it (you know what it represents). You must engage in some incremental manoeuvres if belief is to emerge one way or another. You search, very, very quickly, for relevant given information (on alligators, on their normal whereabouts, on recent events in the neighbourhood, on revengeful students, on recent floods, that the psychology department is tired of rats), then consider some pertinent alternatives (perhaps a Mardi Gras nut, a cat gone berserk, a hallucination), match them against some evaluation metric and so on. You will go through some of the same incremental motions if you hear somebody shouting, 'There is an alligator in the building!' or if you suddenly see a panicky inscription on the blackboard saying the same thing. The form of the input does not matter. The doxastic treatment is of the same type. You do not have to notice the treatment, just its output.

Or look at it this way. What else could a belief track? Forget, for a paragraph or two, your prior intuitions and accept the following stipulations. (1) Rep is a *mental form* iff it satisfies syntactic parameters governing formal operations according to rules. (2) A mental form Rep is *meaningful* (or has intentional content) iff it satisfies intentional parameters governing pattern recognition, concept application, stereotype subsumption, and so on. (3) A meaningful mental form Rep *refers* iff it satisfies semantic parameters such as reference and truth conditions. (4) A meaningful mental form Rep conveys incremental information iff it satisfies incremental parameters. Now the question we want to consider is, why should belief be allocated only at level (4) and not at a lower level?

If it is not incremental information that belief tracks then the next most promising candidate appears to be either meaning, at level (2), or a mixture of meaning and reference, at levels (2) and (3). Many philosophers think that meaning or meaning + reference can assimilate the notion of information we are after. The concept of semantic information, for example, embodies this assimilationist view. But this is not going to work. Illustrations and arguments here and elsewhere[4] show that (incremental) information can be conceptually disengaged from both meaning and reference. (The tactic, as we saw, is to vary/keep constant the latter two while keeping constant/varying the former.) So one has to choose. My point in the last paragraph but two was that if one looks, even intuitively, at the conditions of belief fixation (from perception to scientific theorizing), one must see that those conditions are more likely to fit our incremental parameters than the intentional or semantic parameters. In which case, given what the latter sorts of parameters specify, a belief content must be more than just a semantically valued intentional content; it must also be information.

Then there is the argument made earlier to the effect that from syntactic form and meaning we cannot get to cognitive or behavioural role without additional constraints which turn out to be constraints on incremental information. This is as it should be since, I take it, we want beliefs to emerge from what representations tell an organism about its environment rather than from the manner in which they tell it, that is, the very processes of computing and assembling the representations in question. What representations tell an organism is information, how they tell it is syntax and intentional content under concepts, or meaning.

Given, then, that belief tracks information and its content is fixed, in party, by parameters of incrementation, our next task is to

---

[4] ibid.

speculate a little on what sort of mental programme (CINF-reading homunculus?) might conceivably execute such incremental fixation of belief.

Cogitation

It should come as no surprise that our parametric model of incremental cognition mimics to a large extent a familiar model of inductive (in particular, eliminative) hypothesis formation and confirmation. Instead of hypotheses we have units of incremental information. The mental induction involved in CINF (hence belief) fixation is not necessarily the deliberate, conscious, reflective induction which the scientist or the professional decision-maker engages in—a form of induction which is a matter of trained practice and argument, and which is studied and rationalized by the philosopher of science, the inductive logician, and the statistician. Nor is CINF fixation the sort of induction which, we are told, the vision and language modules engage in when computing and assembling their basic representations, such as visual images and grammatical expressions—that is, the sort of computational induction studied by psychologists of vision like Marr or modular linguists like Chomsky. Our CINF-fixing form of incremental induction is somewhere in between, building on the outputs of modular induction (i.e. $Rep(s,m)$) and in turn underlying and providing the raw material for rationalized forms of inductive argument used in scientific practice and deliberate decision-making. I will generically call this intermediate form of mental induction *cogitation*—a sort of working synonym for 'cognitive issue-handling'. (Thinking, that is, task-oriented as opposed to idle thinking, may be the most appropriate folk-psychological analogue of my notion of cogitation.) Question-answering, problem-solving, decision-making, inferring, among other things, are, then, species of cogitation. Cogitation amounts to the activation and valuation of incremental parameters. To use a somewhat mechanical analogy, cogitation consists in forming, connecting, and moving around various blocks of information in arrangements appropriate to the cognitive issue to be dealt with. In such arrangements, brought about cogitatively, believing is the attitude to that configuration of blocks of information which satisfies the analysis suggested in (A) and illustrated in (B) or (C). As regards content, belief is an output of cogitation.

There is solid psychological evidence that the processes I lump under the label of cogitation operate incrementally, on flexible units of information shaped by issues, contexts, and parameters such as those discussed here. The evidence comes from (post-modular) perception, memory recall, discourse, and communication, as well as thinking itself. There are also rational design considerations which support the idea that an intelligent system ought to handle information incrementally, in flexible blocks geared to the issues and circumstances in hand. I have documented and discussed this evidence elsewhere.[5] So, assuming the plausibility of this account of cogitation and its implication for understanding belief, let us now put the picture together and show that it portrays belief as a central mental performance.

3. CENTRALITY AND PERFORMANCE

What we have established so far is that we cogitate our way to a belief, the way Babeau and Babette did, when we deploy a number of co-ordinated incremental moves designed to specify and aggregate units of information needed to handle some cognitive issue. Belief, I said, emerges as a relation to a configurational structure formed in this process. To understand belief in this sense is to understand it as a central type of mental performance. To show this I need first a very schematic portrait of the cognitive mind.

A trilateral portrait of the mind

Let us imagine that there are three major functional components of the cognitive mind which play a role in our understanding of belief. I will call them the Representer, the Centre and the Memory. The Representer is responsible for the formation or construction of various sorts of cognitive representations, from perceptual (in various modalities) to linguistic and imagistic. We can think of the Representer as being made of a number of computational modules. The best known are the vision and language modules. What the Representer does, in general, is to take the proximal input in some physical form and assign a syntactic structure and an intentional content to it, in some appropriate code, according to specific rules and instructions. The result, a representational output of the form $Rep(s,m)$, is something that the Centre can then understand, 'read' for specific information and utilize for various purposes. Whereas

[5] ibid.

the Representer's processes, called *computations*, have the task of assembling basic formal representations, the Centre's undertakings, called *cogitations*, such as thinking, inferring, and the like, operate on, and with, already formed representations, putting them to various cognitive and behavioural uses. The Memory, finally, is of course where representations produced by the Representer and handled by the Centre are stored and recalled from.

The strategy of the argument from now on is to show that the Centre alone can cogitate, hence, fix the incremental parameters required for CINF and belief, and that this cogitative fixation is a matter of performance. Let us think again in terms of homunculi or some such programme-personalizing devices. Imagine that there is a Cogitator which is responsible for the incremental fixation of CINF. Given what the Cogitator has to do and the resources it must exploit, it makes intuitive sense to hold that the Cogitator inhabits the Centre. That would make belief, the output of cogitation, a central mental phenomenon. But there is more than intuition supporting the mental centrality of belief. In different contexts, Stich and Fodor have both argued that belief can only be central in the sense that some of the basic properties of belief, such as inferential interaction, conscious accessibility, indifference to causal origin and to the specificity of the sensory input, access to various sources of information available in the system, and so on, can only have extension at the central, post-modular level.[6] These arguments, which I shall not repeat here, seem quite compelling to me. While assuming them to make the case for the centrality of belief, via the centrality of cogitation, I want to go further and, in section 4, argue to the same effect by elimination, that is, by showing that it does not make much sense to attribute believing either to the Representer or to the Memory, or to construe believing as a general underlying disposition. So we can enter, as motivated, the premiss that the Cogitator is central, fixes CINF, and, when other conditions are met, also manufactures belief at a central level.

What about belief as performance? Intuitively, the elements are already in place for showing this. Alerted by a particular cognitive issue, the Cogitator must *delineate* (or *retrace*) a theme, *activate, select,* and *retrieve* relevant portions from the memory knowledge as

[6] See S. P. Stich, 'Beliefs and Subdoxastic States', *Philosophy of Science,* 45 (1978), 499–518; J. A. Fodor, *The Modularity of Mind* (MIT Press, 1983).

given information, *identify* the area where new information is needed, *have access to* and/or *project* several competing candidates for the new information, *activate* and *consult* the relevant evaluation metric, *accept* a particular candidate for the new information, and *integrate* it into the given information. The italicized words refer to processes the Cogitator deploys. As I have suggested, some of these processes can be construed as enabling the Cogitator to assign CINF to (or read CINF into) the various mental representations assembled for this purpose. These are occurrent, context-driven processes, and so must their assignment (reading) of an informational structure be. In deploying these processes, the Cogitator forms a configuration out of the various (input, memory, etc.) representations it 'reads' for information. The configuration is the outcome of the incremental processes italicized above. In this sense, the overall configuration of states which the Cogitator brings together when CINF fixing is (what I call) a performance or occurrent output state.

Since belief is an output of CINF fixing, it too should be characterized as a performance state of the central mind. The characterization itself must be understood as a *principled* or *type*-characterization. In other words, I am not merely saying that a belief token should be construed as a datable, contextual, occurrent mental structure. I am also saying that our very understanding of the notion of belief, as a mental type, requires a performance conceptualization of some sort. Specifically, my argument has been that in order to type identify a set of information-carrying mental representations *as* a belief we have to appeal to an aggregate set of incremental parameters (as mental types themselves) whose joint valuation is occurrent and contextual, and can only be construed as some sort of performance state of some appropriate mechanisms or devices, such as the Centre, and, in particular, the Cogitator. Specific belief tokens, then, are going to be individuated by the specific aggregate values of such parameters.

This account of belief as a performance state does not entail construing belief as a type of action or process or happening or activity or doing. What I suggest, rather, is that we think of belief as a functional and configurational sort of output state which the central mind occupies only when certain parameters (of incremental cognition) are *activated* or *valued*, something which happens only when certain sub-components and processes of the mind jointly enter into some appropriate states. The general idea, there-fore, is to type-construe belief content as a function of several parameters (of incrementation) whose joint valuation specifies an entire configuration of representational states. Belief remains a relation to a configuration of representations. The points that are being made are, first, that it takes such a configuration to specify the informational content of a belief and, second, that the specification itself is a matter of occurrent 'reading' of the relevant represen-tations by the central mind.

So far the argument has gone like this: there is a plausible parametric model of CINF fixation; CINF is part of the belief content, for it is functionally efficacious in cognition and behaviour; the parameters of CINF fixation can be shown to be parameters of belief; but those parameters are activated only by cogitation, hence in a certain sort of performance; therefore, belief must be a sort of performance state of the mind. There is another, somewhat dif-ferent, way of reaching the same conclusion. It takes as its starting point the mental centrality of belief, a proposition which has been premissed earlier and to which I shall give further support in section 4. This new route exploits the notion that the central mind is nothing but the theatre of complex and occurrent aggregations and interac-tions of cognitive processes and states which can only be understood in terms of performance. Therefore, if belief is a creature of the central mind, it must be a sort of performance state.

One way of making the argument is by going back, for an analogy, to the good old view of belief as conscious experience. Suppose, contrary to your better judgement, that the good old view is right. Then, I say, belief must be a sort of mental performance state because so is consciousness. You can think of the latter, on the model of attention, as some sort of accessing, reading, and monitor-ing of representations. These are all occurrent relations to represen-tations. If belief is a conscious experience of some sort, then it must be the output state of such occurrent relations. Disconnect con-sciousness and those relations of access, reading, and monitoring cease to exist. And so does believing. So believing must be an occurrent sort of relation. To enlarge the picture, remember what the view of believing as consciousness competes with. One com-petitor is the notion of unconscious belief. This is a viable com-petitor of the view of belief as consciousness but not of the view of it as *performance*. For what the latter allows, as I think it should, is that the accessing, reading, and even monitoring can take place without consciousness. If those operations are needed to fix belief, then belief can be an output of unconscious mental performances.

Although I do not think that the view of believing as consciousness is right, it does point to something important. There are circumstances (sleep, incapacitation, lack of attention, etc.) when the central mind does very little, if anything at all. Does the system believe anything under those circumstances? Even if some memory representations are explicitly stored as beliefs, a possibility we shall discuss later on, I do not think we can say that it does. Storing beliefs is not yet believing. The reason should be obvious by now. Without an appropriate context of incremental cognition nothing is being believed, for no incremental information is being fixed without cogitation, and in the circumstances we are talking about there is no cogitation.

Let us consolidate what has been said so far by weakening competing views.

4. WHAT BELIEVING IS NOT

Philosophers have said or implied many things about belief. Three, however, stand out as perhaps the most popular and resilient dogmas about belief. One is the dispositional, another the memory, and the third the registrational, or modular, view of belief.

Disposition?

An excellent characterization of the dispositional notion of belief was given by Ryle. He writes that believing 'is a propensity not only to make certain theoretical moves but also to make certain executive and imaginative moves, as well as to have certain feelings'.[7] In a sense, I could not agree more: believing must presuppose such a disposition if my incremental account is to have any plausibility at all. But the dispositional view does not want a relation of presupposition between belief and the required disposition; it wants some sort of identity. This is why the dispositional view is both too weak and blatantly incomplete. It is too weak because it accommodates too much and therefore says very little which is specific about belief. The dispositional view, in Ryle's very formulation, also fits other

[7] G. Ryle, *The Concept of Mind* (New York, 1949), p. 135.

BF161 .R9 1949

mental attitudes, such as desiring and planning. This is why it lacks the conceptual specificity needed to isolate and explicate belief.

The weakness is not only conceptual, it is also explanatory. Consider the standard counterfactual analysis of belief proposed by the dispositional view: '*S* believes that *p*' amounts to 'If it were the case that *q*, *S* would (do, think, imagine, choose, feel, etc.) that *r*'. For example, 'Babette believes that Pusha wants an ice-cream' amounts, on this analysis, to 'If Babette had money, she would buy Pusha an ice-cream'. If this analysis is meant to be reductive or eliminative of belief (and other mental attitudes), as it typically is, then it is not going to work. The point is familiar, but I want to enlist it here in the service of my position. The fact is that the presumed disposition to act (think, imagine, feel, or whatever) which characterizes belief would not be activated unless Babette's other relevant attitudes, other beliefs too, were brought into the picture. Thus, for instance, the analysans does not explain anything unless we further assume that, in the context, Babette also *wants* to please Pusha (after the Bruckner-related punishment) and *believes* that buying her an ice-cream would achieve the desired result. Further beliefs and desires may be needed to fix these beliefs, and so on. So, even if belief were a sort of disposition, it would not be activated, and would not become cognitively and behaviourally efficacious, without an aggregation of other interacting attitudes being activated at the same time. But, as argued earlier, this is already a characterization of what is going on as a performance. Saying, by way of analysis, that the other attitudes are also dispositions is not going to help because, even if they were, it is again their occurrent aggregation and interaction, not merely their being dispositions, which have been shown to do the explanatory work. In other words, we have to go from disposition to performance to specify what information a representation encodes and what role it plays, hence, whether it is a belief and what belief it is.

This brings us to the incompleteness of the dispositional view. The view leaves a huge gap between the existence of a mere disposition (which says something like, 'Form a belief whenever the conditions are appropriate', meaning, 'Do *x* whenever *y*, other things being equal') and the fixation of the specific mental content which is going to do the real work of a belief. How is the gap between disposition and content going to be bridged? The dispositionalist faces a dilemma. Each horn of the dilemma forces him to go beyond talk of mere dispositions. The question we are asking is, how does a disposition encode a mental content? The encoding can be either explicit or implicit. If it is explicit, we are really talking of mental representation. We may be talking of syntactic and intentional dispositions to form representations but, as we saw, this is hardly talk of belief. Or, more likely, we may be talking of memory representations, given that the point of the dispositional talk is to emphasize stability and latency of belief. We shall see shortly what this implies. If, as is more likely, the encoding meant by the dispositionalist is implicit or procedural (not a representation, rather a way of handling representations), then he may be talking of primitive or architectural constraints on information processing. But such constraints, it turns out, can plausibly be attributed only to the Representer's modules. In that case, the encoding of belief is modular, not central. Modular belief, I argue, is not a sensible notion. Modular representations are certainly necessary for belief but they cannot be beliefs. Procedures to handle representations can also be acquired and stored. But such procedures only characterize the attitudinal part of a belief, not its content.

To summarize, then: if belief is analysed as a central disposition or procedure, then it is too weak a notion, for it fits many other attitudes, and is explanatorily incomplete, for it does not show how the disposition or procedure encodes the content which does the cognitive and behavioural work expected of a belief. As a disposition, belief will do better if located either in the Representer or in Memory. But this new choice is dilemmatic, as neither component displays genuine doxastic virtues. Let us see why.

Memory?

Memory belief is a tricky topic, so I will try to work in successive approximations. Let me begin with a blunt implication. If belief is an attitude towards incremental information (i.e. towards something specifiable in terms of some uncertainty, some issue, competing alternatives, some background knowledge, and so on), then a belief is stored as such only to the extent to which incremental information is stored as such. But it is very unlikely that memory stores incremental information, therefore it is very unlikely that memory stores beliefs. The main reason memory is unlikely to store incremental information is that, as we saw, the latter is manufactured in a context where a current issue meets available knowledge and resources of handling it. True, most of the latter are stored in memory but they are not necessarily, not even likely to be, stored in the very form or configuration needed to specify the incremental information involved. We store representations and computational resources out of which incremental information can be manufactured in a context, but it is not obvious at all that we store those representations and computational resources explicitly, in arrangements and configurations which *already* specify particular forms of information. There are practical and principled limitations facing such explicit storage. Practically, it is quite uneconomical for memory to store a huge variety of explicit configurations of representations specifying so many forms of incremental information when it is much easier and possible to generate those forms of information when necessary. The principled limitation is this. Incremental information is defined relative to, among other things, an uncertainty to be reduced, some competing alternative, and a pool of relevant data. It is very hard to make sense of the notion that memory constantly stores representations of specific values of these parameters. We may store representations of particular issues or problems and contemplated solutions, in case we have not made up our minds or for some other such deliberate reason, but this is typically temporary. Once we have reduced or eliminated some current uncertainty in a context of cogitation, we move on to other issues. We may, and probably do, retain general procedures of dealing with similar classes of issues (cogitational routines, if you like), but that is still different from retaining and storing beliefs. The procedures, unlike the beliefs, are ways of handling, not representing, information.

So we have a conflict between two powerful intuitions. One is that memory stores a lot of beliefs. The other is that an essential aspect of belief content is information, most likely in something like the incremental format considered in this paper. But it looks as if our current notion of memory cannot accommodate both intuitions. One intuition has to go. Since I find the connection between belief and information quite holy and untouchable, I am prepared to let the notion of memory belief go. So my first blunt conclusion is: there are no memory beliefs.

Before I weaken this conclusion, I want to strengthen it a bit further. For memory to store a belief it must store a configuration of representations encoding some information. My earlier argument was meant to undermine the plausibility of the view that memory can store such information by storing the required *configuration* of representations. Now I want to undermine the plausibility of the *antecedent* presupposition that in general memory stores, explicitly, the very *representations* which constitute particular beliefs. This brings us to the question of tacit versus explicit beliefs.

Do I believe that 465 is larger than 2? Now that I ask myself and quickly go through the incremental moves required (or transfer moves made in similar contexts), yes, I do. Did I believe it two minutes ago, before I asked myself this question? How? Explicitly? Not likely. I do not think that the specific representation '465 is larger than 2' (in this or any other form) was ever copied by my memory because it was never sent there. This is because I have never thought of it before. And even if I once formed it (say, one dull afternoon at school), I trust that an efficiency device in my memory quickly disposed of it, as it probably does with most of our very specific representations. But did (do) I believe that 465 is larger than 2 implicitly or tacitly? In what sense? As a potential but never represented implication of some basic truths of arithmetic which I also happen to believe? This will not do. First of all, it is not wise to extend the notion of belief to tacit, unrepresented logical implications, for the simple reason that a content which is not represented in some form is a content which does not contain information, and belief *is* an attitude to information. Second, even if we decide to extend belief, tacitly, to logical implications, as many urge, we should note that the decision is motivated on syntactic and semantic grounds. The notion of logical implication *is* a creature of syntactic and semantic considerations. I have nevertheless argued that such considerations underdetermine the attribution of belief because they are incapable of capturing the information a belief encodes.

So how should we think of my current belief that 465 is larger than 2? My suggestion is: as an occurrently manufactured piece of information whose representation was generated by some appropriate process. We have a recognized ability to generate representations for various purposes, including those of cogitation and action. Why shouldn't we assume that we also generate beliefs out of basic representations under information-sensitive rules and constraints. There may well be procedural constraints (in the form of routines, habits, schemes, and so on) which often guide quite rigidly the manufacture of many of our beliefs about time, space, arithmetic, logical relations, objects, cats, and so on. But this is different from saying that particular, explicit representations are stored in the very form in which they surface as beliefs. It may well be that what we *mean* by 'long-standing' or 'dispositional' beliefs are not explicit, specific-content-encoding representations but, rather, enduring and fairly standardized procedures of generating the representational configurations needed for belief. It certainly looks more rational for memory to work in this way.

The moral of this part of the argument can be formulated as follows: to have a memory belief that p is to store the representational resources and have the procedural dispositions to manufacture the belief that p, occurrently, in some context of cogitation, not necessarily a conscious one. The content 'that p' is of course type-individuated according to several type of parameters, incremental parameters included.

And yet, we may want to say, even though incremental information is occurrently manufactured in the appropriate contexts of cognition, and even though the representations encoding that information are generated rather than explicitly stored in the very form of that encoding, we still seem to store and have long-standing and explicit beliefs. How should we account for them? Here is my line of speculation.

We obviously store much more than we believe. We store representations originating in perception, and in imagining, desiring, or intending various states of affairs. Unless, for some reason, the original cognitive context (perception, imagination, intention, etc.) is itself copied, indexed, or filed in some form, the resulting representations, if stored at all, are likely to be stored without special distinction. In other words, those representations are not intrinsically beliefs or desires or intentions; they are just inert, informationless inscriptions, patterns on the memory disc, as it were. If, however, a representation is stored, since copied or indexed or filed, *as a belief* (or intention, etc.), this must mean that it was initially manufactured as a belief (intention, etc.) in an occurrent context of cogitation. The copy or index is a record of the attitude generated in that context. I am saying, in other words, that a representation is stored as belief only when (a) it is the output of some earlier cogitation and (b) a copy of the attitude formed in the cogitation context or an index signifying 'believe what follows' or some explicit filing in a doxastic dossier or address, accompanies the representation in question.

To illustrate: if I have always believed that $2 + 2 = 4$, it is because the representation '$2 + 2 = 4$' was copied or indexed or filed with a record of the original attitude.This package was later reinforced on many, mostly philosophical, occasions and has become fully routinized. As a result, I now have a vicious disposition to yell '*Yes!*' whenever asked whether I believe that $2 + 2 = 4$. (I wish Descartes' demon would one day do something about this.) Such storage is possible. In this sense we have a number of explicit memory beliefs.

But even this conclusion need not be conceded too quickly or at least not without significant modulation. Even if something like 'BELIEVE (that p)' is explicitly stored, I want to say that what is stored thus is still a sort of virtual belief. A belief is virtual if it is stored explicitly, as attitude-and-content, but *without* an appropriate context of cogitation. When the latter is supplied, given the record of the attitude, the stored content goes more or less automatically into a belief position, without much cogitation. But the context can still make a difference, even for virtual beliefs of this sort. This goes to show that, when stored, those beliefs are just that, virtual, that is, less than actual. The occurrent context of incremental cognition can, for example, make a difference if the competing alternatives change their strength. If the alternative of God's manipulating my mental representations becomes serious, my virtual belief that $2 + 2 = 4$ may require re-evaluation. Silly sceptical games apart, the point I am making is that virtual beliefs must still struggle to become beliefs in an actual context of cognition.

While conceding the presence of a good number of virtual beliefs, I still find it more plausible to think that memory stores the resources out of which beliefs are manufactured than to think that it stores already manufactured beliefs. This line of speculation is not that outlandish. There is good introspective as well as experimental evidence to suggest that, relative to their originals, memory copies decay fairly fast and become simplified, schematic, shallow. It is common observation that very soon after we read or hear a sentence we typically forget its actual wording, grammar, intonation, theme, and informational context, yet retain for a longer time, or are able to recover quickly, its meaning. Quite often, it takes grammatical features such as passive/active constructions, cleft constructions and others, intonation, prior text, and surrounding context to shape the incremental information that is being conveyed in a sentence. The fact that these information shapers are not stored is indication that the information they shape is not stored either. We know this from experience, and there is also ample psycholinguistic literature which shows it.[8] But then, if the specific incremental information is missing, so must be the attitudes that are designed to be sensitive to it.

The point just made suggests an interesting parallel with what Fodor says about the outputs of the Represerter's modules,[9] (about which more in a moment). Fodor calls those outputs 'shallow' in the sense that only their syntactic and (in my terminology) intentional features are computed. It takes the central mind to read more into them, for example, speech-act force or irony or (the most important to my mind) information. It is worth speculating that, special indexing or filing apart, there may be some sort of reverse process through which memory strips the incoming representations of their cogitative ambience and richness, as it were, and stores them as counterparts of shallow outputs, for further use by the central mind. The picture then is the following: when a particular context of cognitive performance provides the occasion, the Centre receives shallow outputs from the Represerter and also reaches into Memory for some more. Given other constraints, the Centre 'reads' both sorts of outputs for the incremental information it needs to handle the issue raised by the occasion. In so doing the Centre 'attitudinizes' the representations conveying that information and makes them into beliefs, among other things.

Modular beliefs?

Does the Represerter, in its various modules, form any beliefs? Are there (such creatures as) modular or registrational beliefs? A familiar, and occasionally useful, strategy, in the search for an answer, is to formulate a number of plausible constraints on the notion of belief (constraints which in fact encapsulate the reasons for having this notion in the first place) and then asking which components of the mind can possibly satisfy the constraints and thus exhibit believing. In some form or another we have already used

[8] See E. and H. Clark, *Psychology and Language* (New York, 1977). I discuss some of the evidence in Bogdan, 'Mind, Content and Information'.

[9] Fodor, *The Modularity of Mind*, pp.

this strategy. At this point in the argument, if we look at a few selected constraints on believing, we must conclude that modular belief is a very implausible notion.

As mentioned earlier, arguments have been put forward (particularly by Stich and Fodor) to the effect that belief cannot emerge at the modular level. The basic idea is that, on the one, doxastic, hand, we expect beliefs to be accessible, consciously or not, to various cognitive and behavioural processes; to be inferentially integrated; to interact with other mental attitudes and thus be cognitively penetrable; to be abstracted from (or not necessarily carrying information about) their causal origin, hence not to be bound to a particular sensory domain; and not to be hard-wired. On the other, modular, hand, the Representer's formation and handling of modular representations, prior to the shallow outputs, display precisely the opposite properties. These representations are inaccessible to other processes in the system; are inferentially unintegrated and cognitively impenetrable; are tied to their causal origin, hence bound to a specific sensory domain; and are hard-wired. That should suffice, I suppose, to exclude belief from the modular theatre of cognition. If a modular representation is a mere registration of some input in the form of a syntactic and intentional structure, then such a registration cannot be a belief. This is not because, as many philosophers would put it, such a registration fails to perform a role or engage an intention, or because it is too lawful to accommodate the idea of false belief, but rather because, as treated at the modular level, such a registration fails to display the sort of information we want to associate with belief. The other failures are symptoms of this 'informationlessness'.

But if you still have reservations, consider quickly these further constraints. You surely want beliefs to be possibly false. Not likely, if they are modular. The modules do not make many mistakes and are indeed fairly lawful at the appropriate (not necessarily physical) level of description. Even illusions are typically excellent and lawful modular accomplishments. When you know how the visual module works and the physics of the environment, the stick perceived to be bent in water is what you would expect from a reliable visual module. If the stick were perceived to be straight, you would take the module either to be faulty in a strange way or else manipulated by the central mind, hence no longer a module. You may also want beliefs to be changeable, revisable. Not if they are modular.

Modules do not really understand this sort of cognitive weakness and hesitation, unless you drug them. The fact that cats are animals which seem to hesitate in doorways goes to show that cats are not (entirely) modules. Pusha certainly is not.

Consider, finally, this important constraint on (what can be called) the maximal specificity of a belief. The rough idea is that, other things being equal, we want a belief to have (be) the most specific information which a set of representations can syntactically and intentionally encode and which makes a functional difference to the organism's cognition and behaviour. Suppose we have two syntactic forms P and Q, of whatever complexity, which are intentionally and semantically equivalent. If Q carries CINF and P does not, then Q is to be treated as a belief, but not P. The implication is that if P is a shallow output of the Representer (or one culled from Memory, for that matter) and Q is its central, CINF-added reading, then Q, but not P, is the belief being fixed in that context, in spite of the assumed syntactic, intentional, and semantic equivalence of P and Q. Since, in general, shallow modular outputs do not by themselves convey incremental information, whereas their central readings do—which is why the latter are more specific than the former—beliefs must be centrally debriefed, as opposed to modularly formed, representations.

In canvassing several serious possibilities concerning the mental realization of believing, that is, components of the mind which could functionally execute believing, we have also constructed an argument from elimination. If belief is neither a mere underlying disposition of some sort, nor originally a memory representation, let alone a modular representation, then (given the alternatives) it must be a central representation assigned an informational structure of an incremental sort. Since, moreover, the central mind is an office where input and shallow representations, from either the Representer or Memory, are read and debriefed for specific information and then directed to do some work, belief must be manufactured occurrently, as an output of these very undertakings by the central mind.

Before concluding with some reflections on this story of belief and some of its consequences, let me speculate just a little on one psychological aspect of the story. Neuroscientists have been aware for quite a while that the brain processes information on many channels at once or in parallel. Needless to say, this makes better and faster processing than serial processing. More recently, cognitive psychologists and workers in artificial intelligence have paid more attention to cognitive models which employ parallel processing. Philosophers have been slower in seeing the relevance of this development. It may not mean very much if one is interested only in, say, the purely semantic or formal aspects of cognition, as most philosophers are. Yet it may mean a lot to one who is also interested in central processes, such as thinking or inference, or, in particular, in the way such processes manufacture information. The assumption of serial processing *may* force the theorist to view each complex representation, such as a sentence or formula, as a self-contained unit fully valued syntactically, informationally, and functionally, hence as a belief. Most philosophers, I guess, tend to take this line. My story of belief, on the other hand, also allows the assumption of parallel processing when it comes to the manufacture of incremental information. The idea is that the CINF-manufacturing programme may access and read several representations at once in order to extract the needed information. None of these contributing representations by itself, not even the principal input representation (typically encoding the new information), is a belief *prior to* the parallel and aggregate manufacture of incremental information. The didactic upshot of this line of thought is that if we become accustomed to the idea of parallel processing underlying central mental processes, then we may also become accustomed to the idea that it takes several syntactic and intentional forms to fix the information to which a belief is sensitive. This in turn may have the salutary effect of containing the temptation to posit beliefs left and right, whenever a representation (*qua* syntactic and intentional form) is assembled, stored, recalled or operated on. Believing takes more than that. But I would urge this very same conclusion even when we start from the premiss of serial processing.

5. SUMMING UP

Where does all this leave the notion of belief? Well, belief is still an attitude to some mental representations having some formal structure, intentional content, and semantic co-ordinates. It is just that the representations focused on by the belief attitude now constitute a configuration which, when read by an appropriate programme, specifies some incremental information which in turn engages the organism's cognition and behaviour. The argument has been that the belief attitude tracks this sort of information, not just its syntactic and intentional encoding—or rather tracks the last two only *in so far as* they carry some incremental information. So, on my account, one still believes the good old 'that *p*' when one believes something. It is just that the type-identity of what the *p* in question stands for is no longer a mere syntactic and intentional object which is semantically valued, as the standard notion has it; the type-identity of *p* (i.e. of what is believed) is now shaped by an additional dimension, the informational one.

There is one disturbing challenge with which the informational dimension confronts the philosophical notion of belief. The reader must have detected the challenge from the very beginning, but only now are we in a position to state and defend it clearly. Let me formulate the challenge by way of an objection. 'Haven't you given us all along' (you may want to say) 'an account of belief formation or fixation and not really an account of belief as such, that is, an account of what it is to *have* a belief? Surely, most beliefs are formed or manufactured inductively and possibly incrementally. But their genesis must be different from their intrinsic nature as well as from their continued existence and operation in the mind. You give a genetic account of coming to believe, an account with which many would agree. But you give no account of what it is to believe, that is, to have beliefs and deploy them.'

Quite so, I answer. Mine is an account of belief fixation. But, I claim, this is *all* there is to believing, namely, its occurrent fixation. In other words, I claim that you, the objector, beg the whole question. You assume what you have to prove, and what I have tried to disprove, namely, the existence of a principled, explanatory distinction between forming a belief and having a belief. When you have a belief, you in fact form or manufacture its content, even though the procedures used may be standardized and already in place. Beliefs come into existence when certain conditions are met, even though most elements (basic representations as well as procedures) out of which they are manufactured are typically stored but only in a pre-doxastic state, as it were. Do we store thoughts as such? Not likely. We manufacture them when we need them. But beliefs *are*, for the most part, thoughts with functional obligations. If you think of beliefs which are not thoughts, you are probably thinking of procedures and behavioural routines, or of modular representations (i.e. raw registrations), or, finally, of memory representations. But none of these, we saw, are beliefs.

There is, however, a stronger answer to your objection. It generalizes an earlier argument about memory beliefs. Suppose you accept that beliefs are fixed incrementally in the way I suggest they are, given that beliefs represent information. How is it, then, that what is fixed in this way in an occurrent, incremental context of cognition is *different in type* from what is stored in memory or imprinted as a disposition? The type difference, as I have argued, is due to the absence of specific information in both 'dispositional' and 'memory' beliefs. This clearly means that what I say is fixed is type-different from what you say is stored or operating as a disposition. Which one is belief? Once again, the choice is forced upon us by the conflict of two very strong intuitions: on the one hand, that belief is information, on the other, that beliefs exist in some enduring form (stored, dispositionally, etc.). Since what is information for an organism is contextual and ephemeral, the two intuitions cannot coexist. At least not in the form in which they are currently explicated and theorized about. For me, again, the belief–information combination is the winning combination.

The third answer to your objection comes in the form of an exercise in metaphilosophical diagnosis. Its moralistic point is this: let me explain to you the temptations of calling *belief* something which is less than belief. To get to that answer, we need first a synoptic view of what we have been doing here.

The picture of belief that emerges from this paper can be conveniently summarized in Figure 3. This is no neat way of analysing belief but then belief no neat thing to analyse. The key notions, those of incremental information and belief, have been given no explicit definition, for I have none to give. The strategy, rather, has been to let a number of constraints implicitly characterize them. Thus understood, the notions of belief and CINF are a feat of abstraction. But so is any notion. What we do in setting up such notions is to build equivalence classes around factors we take to make an essential difference to the type-identity of the phenomenon we study, in our case, mental content and belief. The five columns in the middle of Figure 3 indicate basic types of factors thought to make a difference to what sort of thing a belief content is. It all depends on how one casts the equivalence relation, both within and across the columns. Putnam, for example, has argued

SAME			DIFFERENT	
Representation			Information	Role
Parameters				
External	Internal			
Semantic	Syntactic	Intentional	Incremental	Functional
causal source	symbols	meaning	theme	inference
input	forms	concepts	issue	intention
reference	computations	sterotypes	given information	behaviour
truth conditions	etc.	recognition schemes	new information projection	etc.
World	Representer & Memory		Cogitator (Centre)	
		The Mind		
W	[S	+ m	+ CINF]	$\mapsto$ r
	Mental content			Role
From			To	
		BELIEF		

Fig. 3

that syntactic and intentional parameters are not enough to characterize mental contents and beliefs, in particular, by showing that semantic parameters *do make a difference*.[10] So more types of parameters have had to be included. In the same spirit, my argument pushes further and suggests a still wider, content-defining equivalence class which also incorporates informational parameters of the incremental sort. The strategy was to show that incremental parameters do make a difference to our type-individuation of belief content. Which is what we have done.

The result is not going to be very intuitive. The reason, very roughly, is this. Belief is different things to different people in different contexts. One takes from the notion of belief what one needs in a particular context. That is to say that one concentrates on one or more dimensions at the expense of others. We can visualize this process of selection of dimensions as one in which one slides the notion of mental content across the five central columns in Figure 3, thus setting up appropriate equivalence classes. In this way the columns selected are going to delineate the aspects of mental content to be considered in a context, hence, what is believed in that

[10] See, e.g. H. Putnam, 'The Meaning of Meaning', in K. Gunderson (ed.), *Minnesota Studies in the Philosophy of Science*, Vol. 7 (University of Minn. Press, 1975), reprinted in Putnam, *Philosophical Papers*, Vol. 2 (Cambridge UP, 1975).

context. For example, if we are interested in the truth or actual aboutness of a belief, we are likely to assume the belief's informational and functional dimensions and focus only on its syntactic, intentional, and semantic dimensions. We then treat belief as a syntactic truth carrier. But this does not mean that a belief is (type-identical with) a syntactic truth carrier. It only means that in the context in question we assume that the other dimensions (functional, informational, etc.) have done their prior work and shaped the belief in question, after which we can consider only the output of that shaping and examine it only in the light of its semantic, syntactic, and intentional aspects. In the same abstractive spirit we may, for purposes of psychological explanation, treat belief as a mental form with causal impact, i.e., treat it syntactically, intentionally, and functionally, while assuming the belief's semantic and informational dimensions. But that, again, does not make belief (type-identical with) a mental form with causal role. And so on.

Suppose we now ask, 'When are two beliefs, yours and mine, the same (meaning type-identical)?' Sameness, we know, is a relative notion. We have to specify the aspect under which it obtains. In the case of belief, these aspects correspond to the dimensions just discussed. You and I may have the same belief in the semantic dimension, either because both beliefs are true or, more concretely, because they share the same truth conditions. Or we may share the same belief in the intentional dimension because we apply the same concepts and therefore assign the same meaning to our belief. This relative (type-) sameness may be secured even when the beliefs are different relative to the remaining dimensions, if we decide to ignore those differences for some reason. The linguistic practice is such that we still attribute, and explain in terms of, sameness of belief even though that sameness covers only one or two dimensions, not others. Strictly speaking, this is less than the whole notion of belief, but we do not care. The practice of selecting dimensions of interest and then parading them as full beliefs is so deeply ingrained that we find it counter-intuitive to be reminded that, strictly speaking, belief is a plurality of dimensions. Thus, you will almost surely find the following argument counter-intuitive: 'Strictly speaking, the notion of belief must contain the informational dimension. But then, two or more people rarely share the same type of belief since very rarely are they going to manufacture the same sort of incremental information, given that very rarely are they going to share the same data base, alternatives, and evaluation metrics, among other things.' The argument seems counter-intuitive because in most ordinary contexts (which is where intuitions are shaped) we choose to ignore informational differences if other dimensions matter more. So, the moral of my story is, not only do we manufacture belief because we occurrently manufacture an essential dimension of belief content, namely, incremental information. We also manufacture the very notion of belief we find convenient and appropriate in a certain context by choosing the dimensions which we think fit that context best.

So far so good. We approach many other mental and wordly phenomena this way. The trouble starts when philosophers, for all sorts of reasons, allow these normal abstractive moves to freeze into programmatic prejudices which explicate belief. This is when belief gets conceptually assimilated to a particular dimension or particular sets of dimensions which happen to fit a certain conceptual paradigm. If introspectible phenomenalism is the fashionable paradigm, as it was not so long ago, then belief is (as a type, no more than) a conscious experience, a feeling, a vivid impression, in brief, a mental representation defined by our access to it. Then behaviourism takes over and, lo and behold, belief is (as a type, nothing but) a disposition to behave, a functional connection between representational input and behavioural output. Central-state materialism becomes fashionable and belief ends up being (as a type, just) a representation-encoding brain state. Now, in the age of language and its philosophy, belief is maltreated accordingly. Since the leading obsessions in philosophy of language are, how does language connect with reality? what and how do words and expressions mean?, and the like, belief itself gets squeezed into its syntactic, intentional, and semantic dimensions, with some acknowledgement of the functional dimension. In ordinary contexts, dimensions neglected are dimensions set aside for tactical reasons. In philosophical contexts, dimensions neglected are dimensions ideologically ignored.

Since many things will change in our understanding of belief, the prudent metaphilosophical moral to be derived from our story is: expect more, not fewer dimensions of belief. If, as I argue, belief is manufactured by the central mind, then the expectation of its multi-dimensionality is not unwarranted. The central mind is not a tidy, well regulated, and well behaved module, so forget about Occam's razor.[11]

---

[11] I want to thank my friends at Tulane and the University of New Orleans, and particularly Harvey Green and Norton Nelkin, for asking tough questions, making many observations and shaking their heads in disbelief.

INDEX OF NAMES

SUBJECT INDEX